THE BUSINESS PRESENTATIONS WORKBOOK

Clark Lambert

PRENTICE HALL
Englewood Cliffs, New Jersey 07632

Prentice-Hall International (UK) Limited, *London*
Prentice-Hall of Australia Pty. Ltd., *Sydney*
Prentice-Hall of Canada Inc., *Toronto*
Prentice-Hall Hispanoamericana, S.A., *Mexico*
Prentice-Hall of India Private Ltd., *New Delhi*
Prentice-Hall of Japan, Inc., *Tokyo*
Simon & Schuster Asia Pte., Ltd., *Singapore*
Editora Prentice-Hall do Brasil Ltda., *Rio de Janeiro*

© 1989 *by*

PRENTICE-HALL, INC.

Englewood Cliffs, N.J.

10 9 8 7 6 5 4

Library of Congress Cataloging-in-Publication Data

Lambert, Clark, 1931-
  The business presentations workbook.

  1. Business communication—Handbooks, manuals, etc. 2. Oral communication—Handbooks, manuals,
etc.
  3. Public speaking—Handbooks, manuals, etc.
  I. Title.
HF5718.L35   1989   658.4′52   89-4034

ISBN 0-13-107518-7

PRENTICE HALL
BUSINESS & PROFESSIONAL DIVISION
A division of Simon & Schuster
Englewood Cliffs, New Jersey 07632

Printed in the United States of America

Dedication

To the early days in Japan. . . .
For Mama-San, Bushido, and
The long journey down the river of life—
To the peak of Fujiyama. . . .
and the continuing quest for fulfillment

Contents

How This Workbook Will Help You Prepare—and Present—Better Business Presentations xiii

PART I: HOW TO PREPARE A BUSINESS PRESENTATION 1

Chapter 1: Building a Successful Framework for Your Presentation 3

THE THREE MAIN CLASSIFICATIONS OF BUSINESS PRESENTATIONS 3

    To Inform 4
    To Motivate 4
    To Persuade 4
    Presentation Combinations 5

HOW TO BUILD YOUR FRAMEWORK: FIVE KEY AREAS 5

    1. Preplanning 7
    2. Attention 14
    3. Interest 15
    4. Desire 18
    5. Action 21

SAMPLE BUSINESS PRESENTATION FRAMEWORK OF AN ANNUAL BUDGET 21

CHAPTER SUMMARY 23

CHAPTER JOGGERS 23

Chapter 2: Power Openers: How to Capture Your Audience's Attention 25

HOW TO CREATE A POWER OPENER 27

    How First Impressions Can be Lasting Ones 27
    What to Include in Your Opener 27

FIVE SAMPLE POWER OPENING TECHNIQUES 27

    1. Power Opener Based on Shock Value 28
    2. Power Opener Based on a Real-World Situation 28
    3. Power Opener Based on a Current Event 29
    4. Power Opener Based on a Well-Known Figure 29
    5. Power Opener Based on an Enigma 29

SUGGESTIONS FOR CREATING POWER OPENERS 30

    Case in Point: Presenting a New Performance Appraisal System 31
    Sally's Sample Opener 32
    Determining the Impact of Sally's Opener 32
    How Audiovisual Aids Can Improve Your Presentation 33

PREPARING YOUR OWN POWER OPENER 33

CONNECTORS: HOW TO MAKE THE MOST OF TRANSITIONAL
PHRASES 34

    How to Use Connectors 35
    Five Tips for Using Transitional Phrases 35

BUILDING YOUR TALK AROUND A FORMAL INTRODUCTION 36

    Case in Point: Marketing Sales Talk 36
    Sample Opening Remarks 36
    Sample Closing Remarks 37

BRIDGING YOUR TALK TO A CURRENT EVENT 37

    Sources for Current Events 38
    Bridging as an Attention-Getting Device 38

HOW TO PREPARE CONNECTING LINKS FOR YOUR TALK 39

    Sample Connecting Link 39

CHAPTER SUMMARY 41

MEMORY JOGGERS 42

**Chapter 3: The Main Body: Guidelines for Preparing Your Business
Presentation** 43

SELLING THE PRIMARY THEME OF YOUR TALK 44

    Sample Main Body 44

PREPARING THE MAIN BODY OF YOUR TALK 45

WHAT TO WRITE: CHECKLISTS FOR PREPARING FIVE TYPICAL
BUSINESS PRESENTATIONS 47

CHAPTER SUMMARY 59

MEMORY JOGGERS 59

**Chapter 4: Power Closes: How to Gain the Commitment
of Your Audience** 61

HOW THE APPLIED CLOSING TECHNIQUE WORKS 62

    Step 1: Rephrasing of Key Points 62
    Step 2: The Power Close Summary 64
    Step 3: Use of Benefit Statement 64

TIPS FOR USING POWER CLOSES 65

FIVE SAMPLE POWER CLOSE TECHNIQUES 65

   1. Power Close Based on Shock Value 65
   2. Power Close Based on a Real-World Situation 65
   3. Power Close Based on a Current Event 66
   4. Power Close Based on a Well-Known Figure 67
   5. Power Close Based on an Enigma 67

CREATING YOUR OWN POWER CLOSE 68

CHAPTER SUMMARY 69

MEMORY JOGGERS 70

Chapter 5: How to Handle Audience Questions 71

HOW TO ANTICIPATE AUDIENCE QUESTIONS OR OBJECTIONS 71

   Preplanning Strategy 71
   At Conclusion of Presentation 72

THE ICE BREAKERS: WHAT TO DO WHEN NO QUESTIONS
ARE ASKED 72

   Ice-Breaker I: The Open-Ended Question 73
   Ice-Breaker II: Motivate Audience Response 73
   Ice-Breaker III: Secure an Active Response 73

THE "PARAPHRASE" STRATEGY 73

   Technique 1: Rephrase Question 74
   Technique 2: Repeat Question 74

WHY YOU SHOULD CONSIDER EVERY QUESTION
AS AN OPPORTUNITY 75

TYPICAL AUDIENCE QUESTIONS FOR FIVE TYPES
OF PRESENTATIONS 75

PREPARING YOUR OWN LIST OF ANTICIPATED QUESTIONS 81

CHAPTER SUMMARY 82

MEMORY JOGGERS 83

**Chapter 6: The Key Point Summarizer: Your Guide for Preparing
All Types of Business Presentations** 85

HOW TO COMPLETE THE KEY POINT SUMMARIZER 85

PUTTING THE SUMMARIZER INTO ACTION: A SAMPLE
PRESENTATION 89

SIX BENEFITS OF USING THE SUMMARIZER 94

CHAPTER SUMMARY 94

MEMORY JOGGERS 95

Chapter 7: Four Typical Business Presentation Examples 97

THE ANNUAL DIVISIONAL REVIEW 98

Category 98
What to Emphasize 98
Pitfalls to Avoid 98
The Framework 98
Forms and Other Aids to Use 99
Background Data for Sample Presentation 99
Sample Power Openers 104
Sample Connector 104
Sample Main body Selections 104
Sample Power Close 105
Sample Questions 105

NEW BONUS PLAN IMPLEMENTATION 106

Category 106
What to Emphasize 106
Pitfalls to Avoid 106
The Framework 109
Background Data for Sample Presentation 110
Sample Power Openers 116
Sample Connector 116
Sample Main Body Selections 116
Sample Power Close 116
Sample Questions 116

STRATEGIC BUSINESS PLAN 118

What to Emphasize 118
Pitfalls to Avoid 118
The Framework 119
Background Data for Sample Presentation 120
Sample Power Openers 121
Sample Connector 121
Sample Main Body Selection 127
Sample Power Close 127
Sample Questions 128

EARLY RETIREMENT PLANNING (HUMAN RESOURCES
PRESENTATION) 128

Category 128

Type 3: The Superiority Syndrome 185
Type 4: The Very Important Person 187
Type 5: The Chronic Complainer 188
Type 6: The Authority Figure 189
CHAPTER SUMMARY 191
MEMORY JOGGERS 191

Chapter 12: The Coach Approach: Four Steps to a Better Presentation 193
STEP 1: SELECT A TOPIC FOR YOUR PRACTICE TALK 194
Suggested Topics 194
Decide Where to Give Your Talk 194
STEP 2: CHOOSE A COACH AND REVIEW THE CRITIQUE
PROCEDURE 194
How to Complete the Coach Evaluation Checklist 195
Why a Coach Is Your Best Review Method 197
STEP 3: GIVE YOUR TALK AND HAVE IT CRITIQUED 197
STEP 4: COMPLETE THE CHECKLIST FOR PERSONAL IMPROVEMENT . 202
HOW TO ANALYZE AUDIENCE REACTION 202
PUTTING THE FOUR STEPS TO WORK FOR YOU 204
POST-GRADUATE CHECKLIST 204

Chapter 13: How to Deliver a Winning "High-Tech" Presentation 207
HIGH-TECH AUDIO-VISUAL LOGISTICS 207
SERVICE BUREAUS VS. IN-HOUSE PRODUCTION 208
MASTER ACCOUNT TRACKING SYSTEM (MATS) 210
CATEGORY 210
WHAT TO EMPHASIZE 210
PITFALLS TO AVOID 210
THE FRAMEWORK 211
FORMS AND OTHER AIDS TO USE 212
BACKGROUND DATA FOR SAMPLE PRESENTATION 213
SAMPLE POWER OPENERS 214
SAMPLE CONNECTOR 214
SAMPLE MAIN BODY SELECTIONS 214
KEY POINT SUMMARIZER 216
SAMPLE POWER CLOSE 220
CHAPTER SUMMARY 220

**Chapter 10: How to Use Audio-Visual Aids to Enhance Your
Presentation** 165

THE FLIP-CHART 165

Advantages 166
Disadvantages 166

THE BLACKBOARD 166

Advantages 166
Disadvantages 166

35mm SLIDES 166

Advantages 167
Disadvantages 167

OVERHEAD PROJECTOR 167

Advantages 168
Disadvantages 168

16mm FILM 168

Advantages 168
Disadvantages 168

VIDEOTAPE 169

Advantages 169
Disadvantages 169
Six Helpful Hints in Front of the Video Camera 170

AUDIO RECORDINGS 172

Advantages 172
Disadvantages 172

HOW TO PUT AUDIO-VISUAL AIDS TO WORK
IN YOUR PRESENTATION 172

HOW TO USE THE AUDIO-VISUAL CHECKLIST 173

CHAPTER SUMMARY 176

MEMORY JOGGERS 176

Chapter 11: The Art of Handling Disruptions 179

THREE GUIDELINES FOR HANDLING DISRUPTIONS 180

CHARACTERISTICS OF PROBLEM PARTICIPANTS AND STRATEGIES
FOR DEALING WITH THEM 182

Type 1: The Chatterbox 182
Type 2: The Overly Dependent Person 184

Contents

What to Emphasize 128
Pitfalls to Avoid 128
Framework 129
Background Data for Sample Presentation 130
Sample Power Opener 135
Sample Connector 135
Sample Selection from Main Body 135
Sample Power Close 135
Sample Questions 136

CHAPTER SUMMARY 136
MEMORY JOGGERS 136

PART II: BUSINESS PRESENTATION TECHNIQUES **139**

Chapter 8: Tips on Improving Your Presentation Techniques 141

THE WARM-UP TECHNIQUE 141

Three Benefits of Repeating a Person's Name
    When Introduced to Him 142

HOW TO REDUCE ANXIETY LEVELS 143

Nine Easy Steps to Controlling Pretalk Jitters 143
How to Use the SFETS Method to Help Minimize Tension 144

HOW THE "PROS" PREPARE PRESENTATION NOTES 147

Four Reasons Why a Presentation Can Fail 147
Three Steps to a Better Presentation 147
Twelve Ways to Enhance Your Next Business Presentation 151

CHAPTER SUMMARY 152
MEMORY JOGGERS 152

Chapter 9: Body Language: How Your Actions Affect Your Words 155

HOW PROFESSIONAL ROLE MODELS CAN HELP
YOUR PERFORMANCE 155

How to Identify 11 Key Presentation Traits
    Found in Successful Speakers 156
8 Body Language Signals to Avoid 160
Interpretation of Nonverbal Signs 161
Checklist of Appropriate Skills for Follow-up 161

CHAPTER SUMMARY 164
MEMORY JOGGERS 164

FORMS APPENDIX **221**

WORKSHEETS

Audience Research Checklist 10
Guidelines for Customizing Your Talk 11
Analysis of Audience Attention 16
Creating and Maintaining Interest 17
Promoting Desire 19
Moving Your Audience to Action 20
Annual Divisional Review Checklist 48–49
New Sales Plan Checklist 50–51
Marketing Presentation Checklist 52–53
Sales Training Department Checklist 54–55
Outside Marketing Consulting Firm Checklist 56–57
Annual Divisional Review: Sample Audience Questions 76
New Sales Plan: Sample Audience Questions 77
Marketing Presentation: Sample Audience Questions 78
Creation of a Sales Training Department: Sample Audience Questions 79
Feasibility of Hiring an Outside Marketing Consultant Firm:
    Sample Audience Questions 80
Checklist for Preparing an Annual Divisional Review 107–108
Checklist for Preparing a New Bonus Plan 117
Putting the Three Steps to Use 150
How to Prepare Your Coach for the Critique Process 198–199

How This Workbook Will Help You Prepare—and Present— Better Business Presentations

This workbook is specifically designed to help you in preparing and delivering a professional business presentation.

Based upon the strategies used by successful speakers worldwide, the workbook takes you through each phase of preparing and delivering a business presentation. You'll find practical forms, checklists, and helpful speaking hints throughout the chapters to help you better prepare for your presentation.

This workbook offers a variety of benefits. It will give you the expertise you need to deliver a professional presentation in a limited time frame. You will find a *proven learning method* of first reviewing short sections of text, reinforcing this via checklists and guides, and then translating this format into your own customized talk. You will be able to accomplish this on your own, without having to attend a formal program on the subject . . . thus saving you additional time and money. Finally, you will experience immediate results toward your goal of more effective business presentations.

The workbook is divided into two parts. Part I explores the "how to's" of preparing a business presentation. Here are some of the many topics covered:

Chapter 1: This introductory chapter gets you started on the framework for your speech, pinpointing five key areas: (1) preplanning, (2) attention, (3) interest, (4) desire, and (5) action. You'll also learn the three main classifications of business presentations—and how to recognize which type of talk you are giving.

Chapter 2: Power openers and how they can help you capture your audience's attention are discussed in this chapter. You'll learn why first impressions may be lasting ones, and what you should include in your power opener. You'll also learn how to make the most of transitional phrases ("connectors") to help keep your audience interested as you progress from your opening statement to the main body of the talk. And, you'll find tips on how to build your talk around a formal introduction as well as how to use the "bridging" technique to tie in a current event.

Chapter 3: In many ways, this might be considered the "heart" of the workbook, because this chapter will help you in selling the primary theme of your talk. You'll find tips on how to prepare the main body of your talk; and, as a special feature, checklists are offered to help you in preparing five typical business presentations: an annual divisional review, a marketing presentation, a new sales plan, establishing a sales training department, and employing an outside marketing consulting firm. You'll find these checklists will be handy references to help you get started in preparing the main body of nearly any business presentation—regardless of whether your talk is on one of these topics or not!

Chapter 4: Power closes and how they can help you gain the commitment of your audience are covered in this chapter. You'll learn the three simple steps to the applied closing technique, and tips for both using power closes and creating your own.

Chapter 5: This chapter covers a critical part of any business presentation—how to handle audience questions. You'll find a preplanning strategy for how to successfully anticipate questions or objections that your audience may have, and three "ice-breaker" techniques for dealing with the problem of *no* questions being asked. Also covered is the "paraphrase" strategy for rephrasing and repeating questions to be sure you've understood what was asked.

Chapter 6: This chapter takes you step by step through the main form of this workbook—the Key Point Summarizer—a handy guide for preparing all types of business presentations.

Chapter 7: This chapter covers four typical business presentation examples: The Annual Divisional Review, a New Bonus Plan, a Strategic Business Plan, and Early Retirement Planning. You'll learn what to emphasize, pitfalls to avoid, how to set up the framework, and forms and other aids to consider using. Background data for the sample presentation is then given, along with a filled-out version of the Key Point Summarizer for each sample business presentation. The topics chosen for this chapter represent a broad spectrum of "typical" business situations, and are designed to help you in preparing for your own talk.

Part II of this workbook concentrates on the business presentation techniques you should be aware of.

Chapter 8: This chapter offers tips on how to improve your presentation techniques, featuring such topics as how to reduce anxiety levels, nine easy steps to controlling pretalk jitters, the SFETS method for minimizing tension, and how the "pros" prepare their presentation notes.

Chapter 9: Body language and how it can affect your talk is discussed in this chapter. Eleven key presentation traits found in successful speakers are identified and discussed.

Chapter 10: This chapter will help you in using audio-visual aids to help improve your presentation. You'll find advantages and disadvantages given for using a flip-chart, 35mm slides, an overhead projector, 16mm film, videotape, and audio recordings.

Chapter 11: This chapter covers the art of handling disruptions. You'll find three guidelines for dealing with troublemakers, and strategies for dealing with six typical types of problem participants.

Chapter 12: This chapter offers four steps to a better presentation through use of the "coach approach"—a simple but progressive strategy whereby you solicit the help of another to review and critique your presentation technique.

In addition, an appendix is included at the back of the book with blank, reproducible copies of all the forms presented in the text. You'll find this appendix to be a handy source for using over and over for virtually any kind of business presentation.

Chapter 13: This final chapter focuses on how to deliver a "high-tech" business presentation, both from a format and content standpoint.

It's a relatively new addition to the art of preparing and delivering an effective business talk, but one that is now gaining wide acceptance. Using computers to help create graphics and visuals is an exciting new challenge for every speaker—hence, it seems proper that this chapter conclude the Workbook.

How to Use This Workbook

The following suggestions are offered to assist you in making the most effective use of the material:

1. Scan the table of contents, noting the main elements presented within each main sections of the book. Then quickly skim through each chapter to roughly determine the length of time required for you to complete this workbook at your own pace.

2. Select a quiet area where you can study for at least one hour without interruptions.

3. When working through each chapter, make certain that you understand the rationale and purpose for each form or checklist presented. Carefully study all forms and charts used as examples, since they will serve as models for your own customization.

4. Avoid the possible temptation of shortcuts. Even if you believe that you already have sufficient knowledge in a particular area, you should still thoroughly review the material. In most cases, each section of the text is bridged to the next for continuity and additional reinforcement.

5. Avoid long gaps when working through the chapters. It's far better to spend only a few moments each day progressing through the workbook, than reading several chapters at once, at several week intervals. *Continuity of learning* is critical to the degree of competency obtained from this program.

6. Wherever possible, customize the supplied forms for your own use. No one form is really ideal for every type of business presentation, and the more that you can tailor these forms for your own presentations, the more effective you will become.

7. Enjoy the material. The learning process is difficult enough without having an added burden of other time pressures thrust upon you. As new material is presented, continually bridge the text and situations outlined to your own world, relating it to the skills you need to acquire within your own environment.

8. Finally, set realistic expectations for yourself. While one cannot expect to become a really effective presentor within a few short hours, rest assured that by successful completion of this workbook, you will have made an excellent start.

Speech is power: speech is to persuade,
to convert, to compel.

Ralph Waldo Emerson

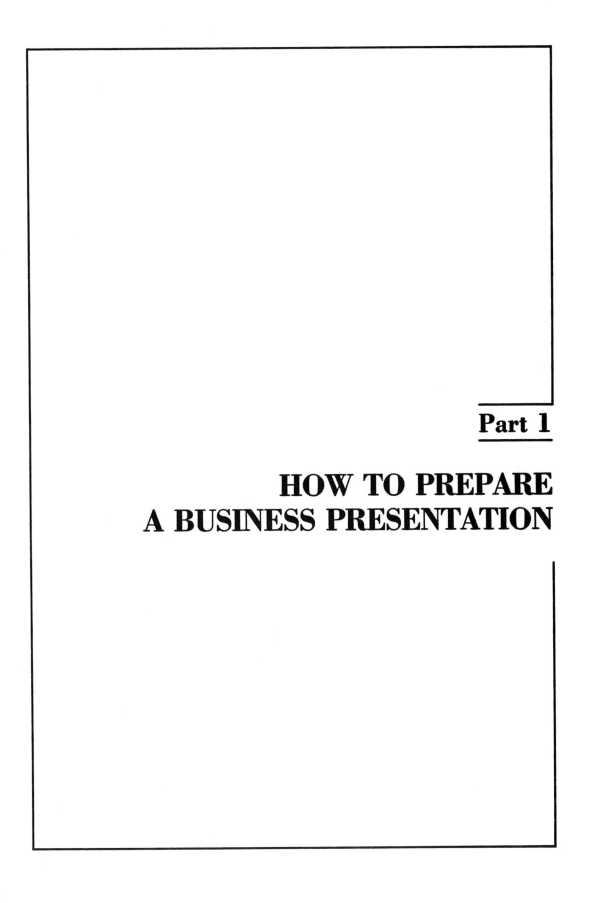

Part 1

HOW TO PREPARE A BUSINESS PRESENTATION

CHAPTER 1

Building a Successful Framework for Your Presentation

This chapter will help you to build a solid foundation upon which you can create an effective business presentation.

It begins by showing you how to determine the type of talk you are giving: one that motivates, persuades, or informs . . . or a combination of these. Once you have determined which classification best suits your talk, time-tested guidelines on preconceived *audience attitude, possible cautions*, and *areas of major and secondary emphasis* will automatically surface. This in turn will lead to the development of an effective framework in which the five following ideas are included: preplanning, attention, interest, desire and action.

The proven presentation techniques found in this chapter are used by many professional speakers around the world. You'll learn how to apply these techniques to typical business situations—with positive and effective results.

The Three Main Classifications of Business Presentations

In contrast to public speaking of a general nature, most business presentations center around three specific classifications:

1. To *inform* the audience of selected facts or figures of a given event

2. To *motivate* a group to take a recommended course of action
3. To *persuade* an audience to your point of view

Let's look briefly at each of these classifications in more detail.

To Inform

An example of a business presentation meant to inform would be a group meeting where the manager of Human Resources explains to key first-line supervisors how the new major medical forms are to be filled out by employees. Your objective in such a speech would be, primarily, to remain as neutral as possible; that is, to be factual, offer the benefits of your new proposal or plan, and keep your comments to the point.

Some sample topics of informative talks include:

- Annual Budget Presentation
- Quarterly Divisional Review
- Announcement of a New Company Policy
- Revision of Rules and Procedures
- New Recruitment Policy
- Handling of Customer Complaints

To Motivate

In this type of speech, you are recommending that your audience follow a certain course of action. For example, you want employees to support the company's annual blood drive. Your audience's attitude may range from passive to positive, though you should not assume that everyone will be receptive to what you say.

Some sample topics of motivational talks include:

- The Need for Greater Productivity
- Fire Prevention Is Everyone's Job
- Why "New Hires" Need Your Help
- How We Can Achieve an Extra 10 Percent in Sales This Year

To Persuade

Persuading goes beyond the motivational speech of recommending; here you are trying to convince your audience of your point of view—and move them to action. For example, a persuasive speech on "Ten Easy Steps for Losing Weight" really isn't successful, unless at the conclusion of your speech you have convinced your audience to try to lose weight using your ten easy steps.

Audience attitude toward your talk can range from passive to extremely negative. You may be confronted with vocal objections or skeptical audience feedback.

Examples of persuasive talks include:

- Advantages of the New Word Processing System—Why We Need It
- The Importance of Yearly Medical Checkups

- Why the New Company Reorganization is Necessary
- The Supervisor's Role in Reducing Overtime
- The Need for Better Community Relations
- Selling the New Retirement Plan

Presentation Combinations

Note that all three types of talks can run in parallel. To illustrate, let's take the case of a company that wishes to achieve a 90 percent voluntary employee contribution rate to this year's United Way campaign. (For whatever reason, last year's rate was a disappointing 58 percent.) As a starter, the speaker would have to find a way to motivate the employees into seeing the importance of the United Way fund and into learning how their contribution, however small, is vitally needed to achieve the 90 percent participation rate the organization has targeted. Once this is accomplished, the speaker has the added responsibility of persuading each employee in the audience to sign a pledge card before leaving the room!

Figure 1-1 is a chart showing strategies to be employed for each of these three classifications. There are four columns:

Column 1, Preconceived audience attitude: Describes the probability of a firm "mind set" (positive, negative, or passive) before your talk

Column 2, Possible cautions: Highlights any possible cautions involved as a result of the preconceived audience attitude

Column 3, Major emphasis: Ties in where the major emphasis of your talk should be highlighted

Column 4, Secondary emphasis: Describes the areas of secondary emphasis that will strengthen the presentation

How to Build Your Framework: Five Key Areas

Regardless of the type of presentation you plan to give, it's critical that your talk has structure. Successful business presentations incorporate five important categories in their framework: preplanning, attention, interest, desire, and action. Each of these five areas has corresponding key points of emphasis that not only provide your talk with the necessary structure, but also provide a smooth transition from one segment of the presentation to the next.

These five categories are also an integral part of the main elements of an effective presentation. In other words, each of the categories has a direct relationship to a corresponding main element. For example:

Category	*Presentation Element*
Preplanning	Covers all five elements (Power Opener, Connector, Main Body, Power Close, and Audience Questions).

	1 Preconceived Audience Attitude	2 Possible Cautions	3 Major Emphasis	4 Secondary Emphasis
To Inform	• Probably passive to neutral	• Do not presume everyone will be in agreement • Some participants may become bored due to indifference	• Be factual • Keep talk crisp • Show benefits	• Remain as netrual as possible
To Motivate	• A range from passive to various degrees of positive	• Don't assume that everyone will be receptive • Watch for possible early negative feedback and be prepared to handle	• Secure early attention • Maintain interest • Heighten desire with use of benefits	• Appeal to, and show advantage of acceptance to talk
To Persuade	• Broad range from slightly passive to highly negative	• Recognize that not 100% of the audience is likely to be convinced • Be prepared for relevant objections	• Keep a heavy focus on advantages involved • Highlight all features/benefits • Show advantage of participant agreement • Always have a strong close ready	• Minimize objections as they arise • Keep building on positive points received from audience feedback

FIGURE 1-1. Strategy Classification Chart

Category	Presentation Element
Attention	Correlates with the *Power Opener*, which secures early attention from audience and builds early rapport. Concludes with the *Connector*, which bridges the Power Opener to the *Main Body* of the talk.
Interest	Begins with reinforcing the *Connector* and develops into the *Main Body* of the presentation.
Desire	Starts with a reinforcement of the *Main Body* (facts, figures, and content) and paves the way for the *Power Close*.
Action	Focuses on the Power Close (or what the speaker expects the audience to do) and concludes by setting the stage for the *Audience Questions* that will follow the presentation.

Figure 1-2, the Presentation Classifications Model, illustrates how these five categories and their key points of emphasis interrelate. Let's look at each of these areas.

1. Preplanning

Preplanning involves all the specific activities that should be accomplished before your actual business presentation. You should try to anticipate any special factors or possible concerns that could affect your presentation *before* the actual presentation. This will help you develop a well-grounded strategy.

Before you begin to prepare the actual presentation, you should consider the following.

Audience Research

- How many people will be coming to hear your talk?
- What are their positions within the organization? (Obviously, your talk will be geared differently to a group of trainees than it would be to the entire executive committee!)
- What do you think the audience's expectations are about your talk?
- Is there a chance that you will not meet these expectations? If yes, can this be corrected?

Customizing Your Talk

- How will your audience benefit from your talk? Have you considered WIFM (What's In It For Me) from the audience's perspective?
- Are there any special factors or cautions involved, such as
  - mood of audience (negative, positive, neutral)?
  - special time restraints?
  - sensitive subject matter?

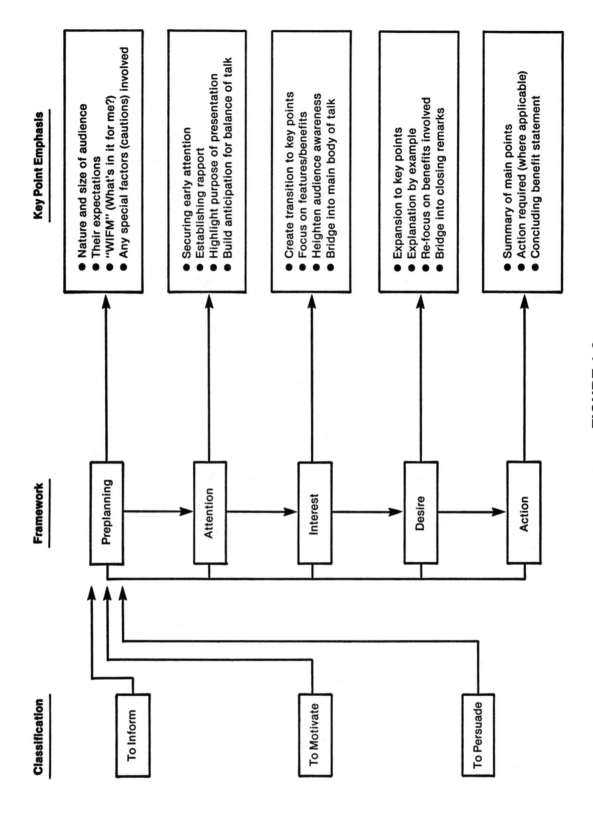

FIGURE 1-2:
Presentation Classification Model

Classification

To Inform

To Motivate

To Persuade

Framework

Preplanning → Attention → Interest → Desire → Action

Key Point Emphasis

- Nature and size of audience
- Their expectations
- "WIFM" (What's in it for me?)
- Any special factors (cautions) involved

- Securing early attention
- Establishing rapport
- Highlight purpose of presentation
- Build anticipation for balance of talk

- Create transition to key points
- Focus on features/benefits
- Heighten audience awareness
- Bridge into main body of talk

- Expansion to key points
- Explanation by example
- Re-focus on benefits involved
- Bridge into closing remarks

- Summary of main points
- Action required (where applicable)
- Concluding benefit statement

8

For instance, suppose your talk was on the new bonus incentive plan for first-line managers. Prior to your presentation, you would want to know:

- Was there a previous plan?
- If so, how was it perceived?
- If not, are there any preconceived notions the audience may have in advance?
- Is this the first time the plan is being presented?
- Are there any "sore points" to stay away from (areas about which the audience may be ultra-sensitive)?
- Conversely, are there any benefits you should especially stress?

Use the Audience Research Checklist on page 10 and Guidelines for Customizing Your Talk on page 11 to help you in these areas of preplanning.

The Room and Physical Environment. A cardinal point to keep in mind here is that both the room and physical environment where the presentation is to take place can have either a heavy *positive* or *negative* impact on your talk. The Pretalk Room Checklist is a convenient checklist that can be used in a variety of situations before an actual business presentation. A filled-in sample of the Pretalk Room Checklist is shown on page 12. In actual practice, it would take only a few moments to complete all of the items in the form, and the time spent will be well worth your effort. Note that the form is divided into three main categories:

Part I: Environment/Room Layout

Part II: Audiovisual Equipment

Part III: Miscellaneous

By using this checklist, you can quickly identify specific areas that require remedial action before your talk begins. Space has been provided in each area for you to write in additional items of importance to your presentation.

Chapter 10 discusses audiovisual aids in detail. As part of your preplanning, you should be aware of the type of audiovisual equipment that is available for your use. It is critical that you know *before* your talk whether or not the overhead projector is working!

Speaker Tips:

Seven Reasons Why Audiovisual Can Improve Your Talk

- Most people in the audience are "TV oriented" and relate favorably to the use of color and motion.
- Audiovisual adds interest to the subject matter.
- It provides a natural transition from you to the overhead transparency, slide, film, etc.

Audience Research Checklist

Who is attending your talk?

Approximate number of people expected:

Educational background and business expertise of audience (if known), and how you think this information may affect your talk:

What specific audience concerns will you be addressing?

How familiar do you expect the average person in the audience to be with your topic?

How well known are you to your audience?

Degree to which you may first have to "prove yourself" before becoming accepted:

The primary reason the audience is attending:

Is the audience coming to your talk willingly or because it's mandatory?

How well do you believe audience expectations will be fulfilled through your presentation?

What is the anticipated length of talk? Should you lengthen or shorten it based on the audience expectations listed above?

Other:

Guidelines for Customizing Your Talk

What is the primary WIFM (What's in it for me) from the audience's perspective? That is, what personal benefits will each person in the audience derive from your talk?

Will everyone in the audience benefit, or just a few? How can you expand the benefits?

List at least five benefits you believe the audience will receive from your presentation:

List five concerns you anticipate the audience will have. How can you customize your talk to offset these concerns and satisfy WIFM?

List any appropriate local current events taking place that you may be able to include in your talk (for example, the thirtieth anniversary of the company founding, a major milestone in the history of the surrounding town).

If your talk is not currently customized for the specific audience, how much time, effort, and money do you think will be needed to accomplish this?

FORM 1.   PRETALK ROOM CHECKLIST

Location/Date of Presentation: *3rd Floor Auditorium Corporate Headquarters 7/18/88*   **Today's Date:** *7/12/88*

Item	Yes	No	Comments
Part I—Environment/room layout Can be controlled by speaker?			
• Heating		X	*Centrally controlled by building*
• Air Conditioning		X	*maintenance. Will check with them*
• Ventilation (blowers)		X	*tomorrow. Already scheduled this*
• Lighting			
– Direct	✓		
– Indirect		X	*Adjusted by maintenance prior to presentation*
– On podium	✓		*Excellent control panel. All functions*
– In main seating area	✓		
• Will a podium be used?	✓		
– Table		X	*(Not necessary)*
– Standing lectern	✓		*Have already made request for this unit*
– Other?		X	
• Acoustics satisfactory?	?		*Need to follow up (but assume it is)*
• Is audience seating arrangement suitable for your talk? (i.e., auditorium style, U-shaped, individual tables, schoolroom style, etc.)		X	*Must revise talk to become more pro-active (heavier audience participation) (See below)*
– If not, what can be done about it?			*Prefer small circular tables (to enhance audience participation) but this can't be done*
• If required, is a public address system available?	✓		*Excellent PA system*
– Microphones	✓		*Both available*
– Lavalier microphone	✓		
Part II—Audiovisual logistics • Equipment source – Being supplied by instructor, and/or in-house facility?			*All required equipment being supplied in-house. •Screen •Overhead projector •2 standing floor easels / pointer*

FIGURE 1-3:
Pretalk Room Checklist (Filled-in Sample of Form 1)

FORM 1. (Continued)

Location/Date of Presentation: 3rd Floor Auditorium Corporate Headquarters 7/18/88 **Today's Date:** 7/12/88

Item	Yes	No	Comments
– If supplied by outside vendor, • Is equipment insured			Not applicable. Being supplied in-house
• Will it be delivered in sufficient time to check-out properly?	✓		Will set up in room approximately 2 hours before presentation
• Can equipment be operated by the speaker, or is a trained technician required? Other?			I can operate equipment
• Audio-visual aids – Being prepared in-house?		X	
– By an outside firm?	✓		Hartley AV, Ltd.
– Chance to review before presentation?	✓		Should be delivered tomorrow (7/13/18)
– Have all visuals been selected?	✓		With exception of 3 flipcharts drawn during talk, all over heads have been selected to meet presentation requirements
– To match the specific presentation requirements?	✓		
Part III—Miscellaneous • Liaison resource – Person to contact for assistance	✓		George Barnes (AV coordinator) or Jan Langley (Program assistant)
– Availability before and during talk	✓		Both people available at all times
• Food source – Name of person coordinating	✓		Jan Langley
– Any special restrictions necessary?		X	Only food served is coffee break at 10:30. Presentation to conclude before lunch
• Need for smoking/non-smoking sections?	✓		No smoking allowed in auditorium
• Other factors	✓		Jan Langley to handle. Needed for
– Directional signs (2) on main floor			directions to auditorium

FIGURE 1-3:
(Continued)

Speaker Tips (continued):

> - Audiovisual aids make your presentation easier to deliver with the help of bullet points, crisp sentences, and color variations.
> - Audiovisual slides and transparencies are generally inexpensive to produce and portable (easily carried with you), regardless of where the talk will be delivered.
> - Effective audiovisual aids hold audience attention for longer periods of time.
> - Most audiovisual aids are very simple to use.

Attention

Since the first few moments of your presentation are critical to its overall success—or failure—you should plan to introduce an early attention-grabbing statement *within the first minute of the presentation*. This type of statement can be relatively short, perhaps three to six minutes. It should be designed to make your audience interested in hearing more. When done successfully, it includes establishing audience rapport (by helping to "win them over" to your side) and then highlighting the purpose of your talk. Finally, the attention phase should embody a short "interconnect" statement that describes the heart of your talk in such a way as to create anticipation from the audience to hear more.

> ## Speaker Tips:
>
> - The audience will form an impression of you within the first few minutes of the presentation.
> - Within the next five minutes, in 90 percent of the time, the audience will reinforce its earlier opinion. Thus, if the audience liked you during the first few minutes, that positive reaction will be reinforced within the next few minutes of your talk. Unfortunately, the reverse also holds true.
> - Make the first few moments count!

Here is an example of the attention-grabbing technique in action. Let's assume that you are presenting a one-hour talk on time management. Through preplanning, you learned that you will be introduced as one of the "leading experts in the field" in the area of managing one's time. Knowing this, your attention-getting statement could go something like this:

"Well . . . thanks, Frank, for that very flattering introduction. I'm probably not the leading expert in the time management field, but in the next 60 minutes, I plan to demonstrate how each of you could become 25 percent more efficient in managing your desk! By

following just a few simple guidelines, that means the average person in this room could save up to two hours each day! How's that for a challenge?"

Speaker Tips:

Attention-getting statements are usually most effective when they

- are preplanned
- can be tied into a speaker's introduction
- relate to a current event
- are kept short and simple

The worksheets on the following pages will help you in successfully grabbing your audience's attention up front—and keeping it.

3. Interest

It's not enough to grab your audience's attention; you must also plan to keep it. Here are ten suggestions for maintaining and heightening audience interest.

1. Use transitional phrases to move from one key point to another.
2. Emphasize the benefits or positive aspects of your presentation.
3. Heighten audience awareness.
4. Bridge into the main body of your talk using connectors. (See Chapter 2.)
5. Keep sentences short and crisp.
6. Use benefit statements whenever possible, i.e., "You will benefit three ways from our revised promotion plan."
7. Always reinforce WIFM when you have the opportunity.
8. Modulate your voice frequently (speak softly, then louder, etc.).
9. Pause occasionally for greater effect.
10. Use audiovisuals to their fullest extent.

Here's an example. Joe Smyth presented the monthly budget review for the Management Committee. This group was a body of eight key executives of the firm, who (during the course of the one-hour presentation) were updated in the main areas of plant operation which involved one of the following:

1. Better than budget forecast
2. Worse than budget forecast
3. On target

Joe was able to incorporate the four suggestions for maintaining audience interest through the use of multicolored overhead transparencies. Each of these slides consisted of:

Analysis of Audience Attention

How do you plan to secure the early attention of the audience? (For example, what type of benefit will immediately catch the audience's attention?)

How will you establish rapport with the audience? (Remember that the first three to six minutes are critical. You need to "win" the audience early.)

Briefly highlight the purpose of your presentation, keeping in mind WIFM (What's in it for me) from the audience's perspective.

Tell how you plan to build anticipation for the balance of your talk. (Reinforce the fact that you will satisfy their needs.)

Creating and Maintaining Interest

How will you create the linkages to the key points of your presentation:

- through transitional phrases?

- aided by audiovisuals?

What are the key points/benefits you wish to convey? Have you included any points featuring WIFM? **Are** you certain that the key points and benefits are really on target?

How will you heighten the audience's awareness:

- through careful use of body language? (See Chapter 9 for a discussion on body language.)

- with the help of audiovisuals?

- by asking selected questions to members in the audience? (Chapter 5 discusses **audience** questions in more detail.)

How will you bridge your opening remarks into the main body of the talk? (Remember to keep the **bridge,** or connecting statement, as concise as possible. See Chapter 2.)

- a key phrase which introduced the area (first color)
- several main bullet points showing budget variances (second color)
- a summary statement which gave an overview of the slide and introduced the topic for the next slide (third color)

Speaker Tips:

Use audiovisual wherever possible in a business presentation. It is one of the most effective support aids available to a speaker.

---

4. Desire

At this point, if the *attention* and *interest* phases were handled properly, the *desire* phase should flow naturally. Here you concentrate on building the audience's commitment to do what you are recommending. It consists of expanding on the key points covered in the interest phase, and then, to "drive the point home" effectively, by furnishing as many examples as possible. Following this would be a refocusing on the benefits involved (further strengthening audience desire) and then developing another interconnector statement to lead smoothly into the concluding *action* phase. Here's an example (taken from our earlier example on Time Management):

"So, as you can see, the Time and Duty Log forms the basis of your efficient management of each day's work. By simply recording each of your activities, such as dictating, reading memos, attending meetings, etc., on a half-hour basis, by day's end you will have a complete record of where your time was spent, by percent of day, and how much time was allotted to each activity.

"Keeping this log for two consecutive weeks will show you clearly where valuable time is being wasted . . . and of course, where to apply corrective action. It's been my experience with many groups like yours that time savings of 25 percent or more can be easily obtained!

"Now, completing the time log in this manner should only require about 20 minutes of your time over a typical eight-hour day. Wouldn't you agree that it's a very small price to pay for the next 15 working days in order to gain 25 percent more efficiency during the next few years?

"Now, here is all you have to do to get started. . . ."

Speaker Tips:

- Make certain that attention and interest phase connect naturally into the desire phase.
- A good connector here will add at least 50 percent effectiveness into the desire phase of the presentation.

Promoting Desire

Expand on the key points you listed in the form on creating and maintaining interest:

Give at least three specific examples that explain your key points:

1.

2.

3.

Refocus on the benefits involved:

Connect ("bridge") your comments into your closing remarks:

Moving Your Audience to Action

Summarize the main points of your presentation (include benefits):

State the action you want from the audience:

Give a strong concluding benefit statement:

5. Action

You can now effectively close your presentation following these three steps:

1. Summarize the main points of your talk (including the associated benefits involved).
2. Clearly tell the audience what is requested of them (obviously, this will vary, depending on the nature of your talk).
3. Close with a final benefit statement that will leave everyone in a good, psychological frame of mind.

Let's return to our example of the time management presentation.

"By following the accepted guidelines on time management you will (a) add approximately 25 percent more to each workday without staying at your desk any longer than you do now, and (b) get through your day with much less strain and tension than you have ever done before.

"To accomplish this, I have left a time management kit for each of you, which you can pick up when my talk is over. Each of you can get started on your new time management system as soon as you return to your desks! All you need to do is follow the five simple steps that I have outlined to you, and which are listed in your kit.

"Now, I opened my talk by stating that in the next 60 minutes I would show each of you how to save approximately two hours out of every day. You are now ready to begin that challenge.

"By the way, just to show you that I practice what I preach, this scheduled 60-minute presentation was given in 54 minutes!

"Thanks for your attention and interest. It has been a pleasure talking with you."

Speaker Tips:

Your closing benefit statement can help greatly to either "make or break" your entire talk. In most cases, that closing statement is what the average member in the audience remembers the longest. Make it a good one!

Sample Business Presentation Framework Of An Annual Budget

To illustrate how the five areas of the framework interrelate when planning your presentation, let's look at the following outline of an annual budget.

I. Preplanning

What to Consider	*Sample Response*
Audience (who will attend, how many)?	One vice president of operations Eight section managers

Audience expectations	A full explanation of the proposed 1990 budget
WIFM (from the audience's perspective)	Must show how a 20 percent increase in research budget is needed to maintain competitive edge.
Special factors or cautions involved	Allotted only 30 minutes for complete presentation. Must be prepared to handle objections on budget increase.

II. Attention

What to Consider	*Sample Response*
Secure early attention	Use benefit statement on importance of budget to planned company growth over the next few years.
Establish audience rapport	Thank group for their assistance in supplying numbers on time, and its importance to the team effort.
Highlight purpose of presentation	To review 1989 budget and revenue forecasts for annual operating plan in 1990.
Build anticipation for balance of talk	Stress interlocking of each budget component in support of company objectives.

III. Interest

What to Consider	*Sample Response*
Create transition of key points	Highlight seven steps to creation of budget.
Focus on features/benefits	Show advantages on early review of numbers to meeting operating plan deadlines.
Heighten audience awareness	Give specific examples of how figures were developed.
Bridge into main body of talk	Expand on the required seven steps in developing the budget.

IV. Desire

What to Consider	*Sample Response*
Expansion of key points	Review each step in detail.
Explanation by example	Give several real-world examples of line input.
Refocus on benefits involved	Bridge back to benefits of early affirmative decision.
Bridge into closing remarks	Restate need for prompt decision making.

V. Action

What to Consider	*Sample Response*
Summary of main points	Review key areas where decisions are required.
Action required	Inform group that decision is needed within three working days.
Concluding benefit statement	Thank group for their attention and help in the decision-making process ... which benefits everyone.

Chapter Summary

You have now successfully completed the framework for your presentation. You have identified the specific classifications (to inform, motivate or persuade), you've specified the key points you wish to emphasize in the five framework phases (preplanning, attention, interest, desire, and action), and you've anticipated the audience's preconceived attitude, possible cautions, and major and secondary speech objectives.

Now you're ready to begin work on the five key elements that comprise a successful business presentation: the power opener, connecting links, the main body, the power close, and anticipating audience questions.

Memory Joggers

☑ Most business presentations focus around three specific classifications: (1) to inform, (2) to motivate, (3) to persuade.

☑ When attempting to persuade a group, you should be prepared for relevant audience concerns and objections.

☑ Don't assume that everyone in the audience will be receptive to your motivational talk.

☑ In certain types of presentations, a classification could fall into more than one category.

☑ The three key emphasis points for obtaining action are (1) summary of main points, (2) action required (where applicable), and (3) concluding benefit statement.

☑ The acronym WIFM stands for "What's In It For Me?" and centers around the need for each member of the audience to hear the personal benefits of listening to the talk.

☑ Creating transition to key points bridges into the framework element of creating interest.

CHAPTER 2

Power Openers: How to Capture Your Audience's Attention

Chapters 2 through 5 will show you how to develop and expand on each of the five key elements of a successful business presentation:

- the power opener
- connecting (or "bridging") statements
- the main body
- the power close
- anticipating audience questions

We begin by analyzing in this chapter the essential points required to create a *power opener* that will help get your talk on the right track from the moment you begin. We also examine the technique of developing transitional phrases (*connecting links*) to provide a natural, easy transition into the *main body* (covered in Chapter 3). Chapter 4 focuses on the strategies needed to develop an effective *power close*—one that will secure and keep the audience's commitment to act upon what you've presented. Finally, Chapter 5 discusses the technique of anticipating audience questions, first by examining what type of questions may be asked of the speaker, and then by recommending ways to supply the appropriate responses.

Figure 2-1 shows how the five key elements of a business presentation interrelate.

BUSINESS PRESENTATION ELEMENTS

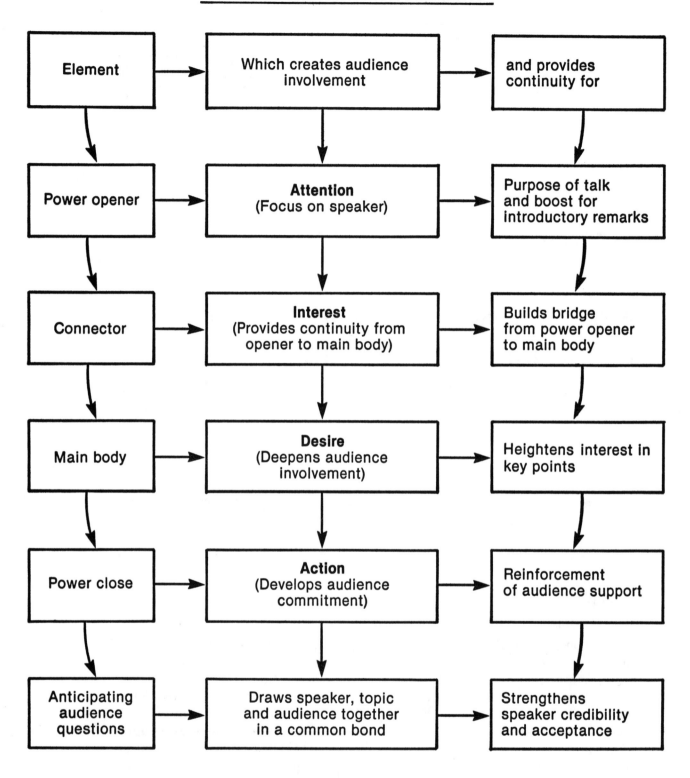

FIGURE 2-1:
Business Presentation Elements

How to Create a Power Opener

The power opener is the initial element that develops the early attention required from the audience. Acting in tandem with the speaker's introductory comments, it also sets the stage for informing the audience of the purpose of the talk.

How First Impressions Can Be Lasting Ones

For professional speakers, it is common knowledge that the power opener (or the first few moments of your talk) can make or break the presentation in the minds of the audience. This is based on the fact that the average listener (upon first seeing and hearing you) forms either a negative or positive "halo" opinion of you, usually within the first minute or two of your talk! Worse yet, almost 90 percent of the time, the listener's early opinion is "confirmed" within the first five minutes. That is, if the listener liked you at the start, he or she tends to like you for the remainder of your talk. Unfortunately, the reverse holds true also.

Let's take this a bit further. This early "halo" judgment of you by the audience can be triggered by many sinister types of bias. These biases include such items as having a dislike for short or tall people, a person's sex, background, skin color, or age. While professional speakers cannot control this unfortunate aspect of audience behavior, they can aid it in a positive manner through the effective use of the power opener.

What to Include in Your Opener

Regardless of the topic selected, an effective opener should consist of several connecting sentences (or thoughts) which have been designed to spotlight the *purpose* of the talk, and correspondingly, to develop *attention* for the topic being delivered. While there is no set formula that covers all situations, a power opener should generally contain the following elements:

- An attention-getting statement early in the talk
- Key points highlighting your talk
- Selected words and gestures to help establish initial rapport with the audience
- Use of WIFM (What's in it for me) that the audience will easily relate to
- A buildup of anticipation and a sense of excitement for the balance of the talk

Five Sample Power Opening Techniques

Obviously, because every presentation given is different, it would be impossible to provide actual opening statements for specific business situations. Nevertheless, the following sample power openers are provided as guidelines for the types of presentations you are most likely to encounter in a business setting.

1. Power Opener Based on Shock Value

"Good morning. I'm here today as a representative of the Intra-State Blood Bank, whom as most of you know, supplies over 70 percent of needed fresh blood supplies to the major hospitals within the state.

"What you may not know is that, due to vacations and holidays, many of our regular donors have not contributed recently, and the result is that our supplies are now 80 percent below normal. What does that mean to you? Well for one thing, our blood fulfills the needs of over 150 patients a day who would be in critical danger without this supply. Going a bit further, statistics show that based on the number of people in the audience today, at least 30 percent of you will have one member of your household requiring a transfusion of some type within the next three to four weeks.

"By way of example, since there are fifteen people in the first row, at least five of you will be affected by this. Hopefully, your family will have this life-saving blood when it's needed . . . (pause) but there's a good chance that some people will now die, due to the lack of it!"

Speaker Tips:

When to use shock value in a power opener

- For talks with general appeal messages, or those of not a serious magnitude (affecting the business directly) such as:
  - Need for more effective recruiting techniques
  - Annual blood drive
  - Request for greater community involvement, etc.

When not to use shock value

- For specific talks on direct business/organizational topics
  - Presentation on the annual budget
  - New product introduction
  - Revised 10-year strategic plan, etc.

---

2. Power Opener Based on a Real-World Situation

"Good morning, everyone. I appreciate the fact that 100 percent of our supervisory staff is present as requested, and that most of you even arrived a few minutes early.

"That's a good sign, since it shows your commitment to this organization . . . a faith in our common future that is now in serious jeopardy unless we all pull together for the next twelve months!

"Although our quarterly figures will not be made public until tomorrow morning, I will disclose the fact that due to foreign competition and our rising labor and manufacturing costs, our company could fold within the next six months. In effect, we may have to shut the doors on a business that has been operating for the last forty-six years.

"So . . . we sink or swim together! The purpose of my talk today is to outline those

specific steps required to save the organization, and I am personally counting on each person in this room to do just that!"

3. Power Opener Based on a Current Event

"Sorry to be a few minutes late this morning, and I greatly appreciate your patience.

"Actually, my flight from Detroit was right on schedule, that is, until we made our final approach to the airport. Everything seemed routine until the plane suddenly lurched up and swung wildly to the right. People panicked, luggage flew about, children were screaming, and frankly I was scared as hell myself.

"It was then, on the left-hand side of the aircraft, that we saw a small private plane who apparently came out of nowhere and was on a direct collision course with our 747. If it weren't for the pilot's skillful handling of the emergency situation, none of us on the plane would be alive to tell about it.

"Knowing how to deal with emergencies is critical in today's world. And in my talk, I plan to show you why our new corporate program on job safety can help put us all on track— and help us avoid potential disaster."

4. Power Opener Based on a Well-Known Figure

"Good morning everyone . . . thanks for coming today.

"I'm pleased to see that all of our key management team is in the audience. That's good, because it means that I only have to state the bad news about our year-to-date performance once.

"For the past six months, our gross sales have been down 21 percent while industry sales have risen by 4 percent. We have slipped our market share from 16.7 to 14.7, and the latest prediction is that this could be further reduced to 12 percent. Finally, our net revenue from operations has also slipped by 5 percent . . . which is the most shocking news of all.

"Who is to blame? Perhaps all of you . . . but I'll take a note from our president's page when he stated that the buck stops here! What does that mean to you?

"It means, that while I hold myself responsible for the alarming mess our company is now in, I'm going to count on each of you to turn this organization around! Can I rely on you? Are you with me?"

Speaker Tips:

Use statistics in a power opener sparingly, unless it's a talk on a budget and numbers will be the primary topic of conversation.

---

5. Power Opener Based on an Enigma

"Thanks for that very warm welcome.

"I'm pleased to chat with all of you today on the subject of heart disease prevention . . . a topic I know is of high interest around the country. Further, if I could speak with each of

you individually, I'm sure you would tell me how important good health is for you and your entire family.

"What you are probably not aware of is that most of you over 35 years of age are probably in the high-risk category, by allowing yourself a high cholesterol diet, and not exercising regularly at least four times a week.

". . . That means that for some of you, you are literally eating your way right into the grave!

"Our company's insurance program has offered us a unique plan to cut costs and promote the general health of our employees. Here's what they have proposed. . . .

Note: Each one of these power openers was preselected by the speaker to fit the occasion. While there are no hard and fast rules on when to use each type of power opener, the safest guideline to follow is one of common sense. What you are doing here is attempting to get the audience's attention through a direct, *appropriate* tie-in. The word appropriate is key here . . . *both to the audience and the topic.* For example, in our first illustration (based on shock value) while the speaker was on safe ground in using it to increase blood donations, shock value may be quite *inappropriate* in presenting the new bonus plan to key managers!

Speaker Tips:

- Always have a back-up approach when employing the power opener. If your planned WIFM doesn't work, have an alternate statement to make. However, if the first technique *does* work, use the back-up as a reinforcer to heighten interest.
- Always *know the audience*!

Suggestions for Creating Power Openers

Power openers for business situations are often found in everyday occurrences. Consider the following ten examples when preparing the opener for your talk.

1. Name three stories that have been in the headlines for the past three months. (For example, special congressional hearings, a presidential election, federal budget deficit or overspending.) Tie in to your presentation.

2. Think of a well-known personality in politics, sports, human rights, or your particular business field. Consider quoting the well-known person or using a specific event to introduce your talk. For example, at World Series time it might be appropriate to use the win/lose theme in a motivational speech on why the new personnel program should be supported because "we're all part of the same team."

3. Name a trend in popular culture and note how quickly it rose from

obscurity to fame to obscurity again. (Examples: pet rocks, hairstyles for men and women, mini skirts.)

4. Observe how "everything old is new again" in many facets of popular culture: the mini-skirt, for example, has become fashionable again in the eighties after the sixties-craze gave way to a more subdued seventies.

5. Tie in an appropriate recent situation to reinforce your talk. For example, if you were caught in heavy traffic on the way to giving the speech on time management, stress the concept of properly planning your day for maximum efficiency! (In this case, you allow yourself an extra twenty minutes for the traffic jams.)

6. Where possible, draw parallels to your talk from outside sources. For instance, if you were speaking on the need for greater productivity, try to draw parallels with similar industries outside of the United States . . . such as Japan or Germany.

7. Always be conscious of current events and how they could impact on your power opener. Especially important here would be something you observed the day before—or, even more effective—a story you had seen on television or heard on the radio the very morning of your talk.

8. Remember to draw upon the unusual as a source for power openers. For example, "bits of wisdom" as relayed to you from a child, senior citizen, or someone not connected to your business could be a rich fund for ideas.

9. Finally, when the situation permits (such as speaking to a group of less than twenty people) use the "feedback technique" to reinforce the power opener. It works in the following way:

- Try to create a challenge to the group in the middle of the "opener."
- Wait for a response from someone in the audience.
- Reinforce this response by completing the power opener.

Example: (on a new production introduction)

- I'm here today to introduce our new model—the X-100 foam car wax, will revolutionize the entire market. Before I begin, however, I'm wondering who could tell me how many waxes of this type are currently available?
- I see from the two responses received that your opinion is between thirty and forty similar products on the market today.
- Actually, the figure is closer to 100! And, in the next thirty minutes, I'll show you why our new product will outsell all of the others by five to one!

Case in Point: Presenting a New Performance Appraisal System

Sally Field is vice-president of Personnel for Jan Fabrics, Ltd., a medium-size importer and distributor of leisure/sports dress for both men and women. She is part of a company management team (including high level managers from all operating groups) which meets weekly on matters of mutual interest.

For several months, in cooperation with other key executives of the firm, Sally has designed a new performance appraisal system to replace the unpopular, out-dated system designed many years ago. Her presentation to the management team was officially placed on the meeting agenda, so everyone was aware that she would be speaking this afternoon.

After completion of several preliminary items, the general manager, Neil Farrell, introduced her topic as follows:

"Well, that completes item number three. Next up, we have asked Sally to give us an overview of the revised performance appraisal system that we have all been waiting for. If anyone in the group could rescue us from the current 'patched-up' version which <u>nobody is happy with</u>, it's Sally. In my opinion, it's one of the highest priority projects <u>that's been going on around here</u>. Okay, Sally . . . over to you."

Sally's Sample Opener

"Thanks very much, Neil. Following up on your comments, for several months now, I've had the 'distinction' of revising one of the most despised company documents in existence! While I don't claim to have created Utopia with the new system, during the next 15 minutes I plan to demonstrate a revised performance system that is both far superior to the current one, and a lot fairer to the employee being evaluated.

"Let's take a closer look at this system which will automatically make you a better manager, and correspondingly raise employee morale to a much more acceptable level."

Determining the Impact of Sally's Opener

Here is a commentary on Sally's opener in which several important steps were done to enhance those first few critical moments of her presentation:

- As a starter, she "bridged" her own initial comments into the introductory remarks made by Neil Farrell.
- She used a power opener based on a real-world situation (the current "patched up" Performance Appraisal System in the company that nobody is happy with).
- The use of the bridging technique helped Sally to launch into an early attention-getting statement, namely, "During the next 15 minutes I plan to demonstrate. . . ."
- Sally made clear use of WIFM with the statement, "Let's take a closer look at this new system which will. . . ."
- Using the attention-getting statement with an effective WIFM enabled Sally to start the buildup of anticipation and a sense of excitement to hear more of the talk.

Interestingly, what Sally successfully avoided (but which is an easy pitfall to encounter) was *not* "jumping right in" to the main body of the presentation without the benefit of a power opener as a springboard. If she had, the talk would not have gotten off to a good start, and might have gone something like this:

"Thank you Neil. Now . . . our revised performance system has six parts with each part having two or three subcategories. All are interconnected through various linkages which provide each employee with a fair rating. Further, we believe the new plan is equitable in that. . . ."

How Audiovisual Aids Can Improve Your Presentation

At this point, it would be helpful to discuss briefly the importance of audiovisual aids in business presentations. Although this topic will be discussed in detail in Chapter 10, it's important to keep in mind at this point that the proper use of audiovisual aids can increase the effectiveness of your talk, in some cases, by as much as 100 percent! By using flipcharts, slides, overhead transparencies, chalkboards or video, you will help keep the audience's interest while supporting the important points you are making. Also, the entire presentation is given a better flow and structure.

The distinct advantage given by audiovisual aids will become increasingly apparent as you proceed further along in the workbook.

Preparing Your Own Power Opener

Here is an example of key summary points used in a power opener. It's taken from our earlier example of Sally Field's opening remarks.

SUMMARY POINTS	VISUAL AIDS
REVISED PERFORMANCE APPRAISAL SYSTEM • Current system despised by everyone • Clearly in need of complete revision • No perfect answer, but next 15 minutes will describe far superior and fairer system for all. (NOTE: Transparency 1 displayed throughout power opener)	TRANSPARENCY 1 • Everyone hates the system! • Why me? • Revision clearly needed • We believe solution has been found • New system far superior and much fairer.

Note that the summary points used in this example consisted of a main heading, supported by several key bulleted points. The visual aids for this section were supported by only one transparency, which highlighted the key elements of the power opener. If more than one transparency were being used, an alternate method of placing information in the VISUAL AIDS section would be to list the transparency number parallel to the appropriate bulleted summary points.

With Sally's power opener illustration as a guideline, you are now ready to begin the first step in preparing your own business presentation. In the space below, write the key points you wish to cover in the opening of your presentation.

In the right column, include any visual aids you plan to use. At this early stage you may not have the transparencies prepared yet or other aids available. In that case, simply write in the VISUAL AIDS section what type of visual aid (chalkboard, video, tape recorder, slides, transparencies, etc.) you wish to use, if any.

SUMMARY POINTS	VISUAL AIDS
1. *Power Opener:*	

Connectors: How to Make the Most of Transitional Phrases

This section examines the importance of connectors: those necessary links that offer a smooth transition between your power opener and the main body of your talk.

You'll learn the four guidelines of the bridging concept and how they help to connect your opening and closing statements with the rest of your presentation. You'll find tips on how to build your talk around a formal introduction and the importance of using current events and other attention-grabbing devices to secure the audience's interest.

In short, you'll discover why transitional phrases play a brief but crucial part in the successful coordinating of your business presentation.

How to Use Connectors

A connector (sometimes referred to as "the bridge") comes into play at the conclusion of the power opener. When used properly, it provides a natural transition into the key points of your presentation, while continuing to build audience interest.

Five Tips for Using Transitional Phrases

Remember that the primary purpose of a connector is to maintain and build on audience *interest*, so that upon approaching the main body of your talk, strong communication bridges have already been built. To do this effectively, here are a few key tips.

1. *Always try to keep the connector short.* The best connectors are never more than a brief paragraph of three to four sentences.
2. *Use of humor or shock value is ideal as a connector, provided what you say is appropriate to the situation.* Do not use humor in a talk based around a grave business situation.
3. *Statistical connectors are usually very desirable.* Remember that the purpose of a connector is to build on audience interest; and it will aid in developing further interest by stating that "65 percent of our existing market will be. . . ."
4. *Use attention-getting connectors wherever possible.* Some examples that are sure to "do the trick" are
   - So, in the next half-hour, I intend to show each of you . . .
   - Yes, we *will* become an industry leader, and we intend to do so by . . .
   - By the way, you have every right to doubt my word, but . . .
   - No . . . I haven't lost my mind. On the contrary . . .
   - Sounds a bit farfetched? Wait until you hear the rest . . .
5. *Use nonverbal gestures when employing connectors.* You can heighten emphasis even further, by:
   - Pausing for effect in middle of connector.
   - Using your hands to make a point.
   - Bringing body language into play; shifting your position from one side to another, taking off your glasses (if you wear them) and carefully placing them on a table in front of you, etc.
   - Raising or lowering your voice for a few seconds.

Building Your Talk Around a Formal Introduction

A key point to consider during the preplanning phase of your presentation is how you will be introduced. If a formal introduction is to be used, in which you will be introduced to the audience by another speaker or by someone known to the group, you may wish to refer back to the speaker's comments in your own introductory remarks.

Here are four time-tested guidelines to observe about the bridging concept following a formal introduction:

1. If possible, meet your introducer before the presentation. This will be a definite aid in increasing your confidence level and reducing pretalk tension.

2. Make certain that you know the content of what will be said in the introduction *in advance* of the talk.

3. Wherever possible, bridge your opening remarks into the introduction. This will create audience interest, heighten enthusiasm for your talk, and help to maintain audience continuity and interest.

4. When concluding the presentation, bridge your closing remarks back to the introduction.

Case in Point: Marketing Sales Talk

Ralph Barnes is vice president of marketing for BMI, a leading producer of industrial air-conditioning/filtering equipment. The product is sold primarily through distributors via the company's six regional offices. Barnes is based in the Chicago corporate headquarters, and will be talking with the company sales representatives from the Atlanta office.

Barnes learns from the introducer (Frank Simpson, regional sales manager) that he is being welcomed as the key marketing executive from the home office—and one who has an extremely important message concerning goals for the next six months. Barnes' talk is scheduled for 45 minutes, and will provide an overview of both the revised corporate and regional sales goals for the first six months of the new fiscal year.

Sample Opening Remarks

"Thanks very much, Frank, for both the nice introduction and the lead-in to my remarks concerning goals for the first half of next year. It's good to see so many of my old friends again. During the next 45 minutes, I hope to show all of you how the Atlanta region will become one of the top-driving marketing groups within the company—and help support our objectives for the next six months."

or

"Thanks, Frank, for the impressive introduction! But, let's make one thing clear right away. Most of you in the audience have known me for quite a few years. You also are aware that although I may have a rather impressive title, when it comes to achieving company sales goals, I consider myself to be just another sales rep—like yourselves. In my opinion, all of you have the most important job within the company itself! Now . . . let's get right to it."

Sample Closing Remarks

"So, as you can now see, we are counting on the Atlanta office to increase sales by 20 percent over the next six months. By doing so, you will not only be a key thrust in one overall company attainment of goals, but you will also give me a good excuse to come to Atlanta again and have the pleasure of being with the number one sales region!"

or

"Now everyone in this room should have a clear picture of how Atlanta's goals are an integral part of our national sales effort. In my book, that makes you all <u>key marketing executives</u>, sharing this new sales challenge equally with me. Let's work together to make it happen!"

Let's take a moment to consider why Barnes' opening *and* closing remarks were so effective.

On the opening remarks
- Barnes did his homework in advance. He knew exactly what Frank Simpson would say about him.
- Accordingly, he was able to bridge his opening remarks (on goals) directly back to the introduction.
- Words were carefully chosen to stimulate audience interest and build on enthusiasm for the balance of the talk. For example: "I consider myself to be just another sales rep—like yourselves . . ." (and) "now . . . let's get right to it!"

On the closing remarks
In reverse (and in both examples given), Barnes developed a powerful close by first bridging his remarks back to the introduction (the importance of goal attainment), then finishing the talk with motivational phrases such as:

. . . *"But it will also give me a good excuse to come to Atlanta again and . . ."*

. . . *"Let's work together to make it happen!"*

Bridging Your Talk to a Current Event

When no formal introduction will take place, a good idea is to bridge your talk to a current event. In order for this "bridging" to be effective, two conditions must be met:

1. The current event must be easily related to by everyone in the audience.
2. The event must be tied (bridged) into the main theme of your talk.

Sources for Current Events

There are many sources for a current event connector. Here are a few examples:

- National or local newspaper articles
- Significant event that has appeared on television recently (local or national)
- Everyday observance (observed when going to work, during lunch time, etc.)
- Picking up/elaborating on a popular trend affecting many people's lifestyles (jogging, health fitness centers, dieting, and so forth)
- Paraphrasing an event taken from the internal company newsletter or annual report to stockholders

Let's return to the previous case in point with Jack Barnes. This time he will not be formally introduced, but instead must rely on the bridging concept of using a current event.

After the initial formalities, Jack could refer to an article, an overheard conversation, or a recent special on television that focused on the relatively lower productivity rate of American companies compared to their European and Asian counterparts. At that point, the slow erosion of productivity to goal attainment could be easily bridged with a transitional connecting link such as the following:

"Well, so much for national trends. Guess they haven't heard of BMI! Within the next hour I'll show you how we plan to make our goals—and become one of the most productive organizations in the United States!"

or

"BMI has never worried much about foreign competition or the rate of productivity compared to firms overseas. We merely spend most of our time consistently making our planned goals and staying number one in the industry. Today is no exception. Let's talk about how Atlanta will top last year's sales by 20 percent—and remain the leader in overall company sales!"

With just a bit of practice, you can quickly become an expert in this bridging technique. Use of this one skill alone should significantly increase your effectiveness during a presentation.

Bridging as an Attention-Getting Device

As a supplement to bridging your talk to a current event, you could also strengthen its impact by using the connector to "surprise" your audience. For example, let's return to our previous case in point with Jack Barnes. Assume that there are 15 company sales reps from the Atlanta office who are the primary audience for Barnes' talk. Barnes might say something like this:

". . . Today is no exception. . . . Let's talk about how Atlanta will top last year's sales by 20 percent—and remain the leader in overall company sales. And I am now looking at 15

keys that will play a major part in accomplishing this goal. Can anyone here tell me what I'm referring to?"

Naturally, the majority of the audience will now start to pay close attention to what Barnes says!

How to Prepare Connecting Links for Your Talk

To see how a sample connector works, let's revert to our example in the previous chapter on Sally Field. We now pick up her talk at the end of the power opener.

Sample Connecting Link

"As you can see from the summary page which I've just distributed, responsibility for employee performance and productivity will now rest solely with his or her manager. Not only will appraisals now be done every six months (instead of yearly), but we expect every manager to work closely with each of his or her employees from one appraisal period to the next! In other words, for the first time, we are introducing continuity in the performance appraisal process—a key ingredient by any standard of measurement."

In this example, Sally used the connector technique to couple the early power opener part of the presentation (where attention was developed by highlighting the benefits that would accrue from the new system) to the forthcoming main body of her talk.

Over the years, many people have asked me about the necessity of including the *connector* at all . . . and in effect, going directly from the *power opener* to the *main body*. My answer has always remained the same. An effective speaker *could* accomplish this by including the elements of the connector (heightening interest) into the tail end of the power opener. Generally, I recommend against this, since it is merely adding one short step to another, and thereby creating nothing more than one longer step in itself.

Here's an example of a summary of the key points discussed in Sally's connecting link.

SUMMARY POINTS	VISUAL AIDS
2. Connector: MANAGERIAL RESPONSIBILITY •Sole responsibility for performance with manager • Appraisals now done every six months • Continuity ... Key to success	TRANSPARENCY 2 •Expand responsibility for managers TRANSPARENCY 3 • 6-month appraisals instead of one year • Continuity will play major part in success of system

Let's briefly review what Sally did:

1. She used "managerial responsibility" as her connector. This was to be reinforced by transparency #2.
2. To support the connector, note the three bulleted point phrases . . . aided by transparencies #2 and #3.

Note: Depending upon related variables (such as budget/time required for transparency preparation), and the number of people in the audience (which affect the amount of lines that can be placed on each transparency), Sally could have placed all of the information on one slide, or have had a separate transparency for each bulleted point.

Use the space provided to write down appropriate connectors for your talk. Include headings for the visual aids you plan to include.

SUMMARY POINTS	VISUAL AIDS
2. *Connector:*	

Speaker Tips:

- Connectors (bridging statements) are especially enhanced with appropriate audiovisual support. Use it wherever possible.
- Bridging your opening remarks into the introduction (and with the closing also) is a sure-fire way to help keep the presentation lively.

Chapter Summary

With the completion of this chapter, you have learned how to use a power opener to get a business presentation off to a good start.

You have identified the key elements needed to create a power opener, and reviewed five real-world sample power opening techniques (based on shock value, a real-world situation, a current event, a well-known figure, and an enigma.) You've also learned the value of using connectors to bridge the power opener to the main body of the talk, with examples on how to prepare the connectors for maximum effectiveness in front of an audience.

At this point, you're ready to start work on preparing the main body of the presentation . . . the key section of your talk that conveys the all-important theme of what you are attempting to convey to the audience.

Memory Joggers

☑ There are five key elements to a successful business presentation: (1) power opener, (2) connector, (3) main body, (4) power close, and (5) handling of audience questions.

☑ The purpose of a power opener is to grab your audience's attention—and keep it.

☑ The average listener forms a negative or a positive opinion about you during the first few moments of your talk. Almost 90 percent of the time, the listener does not sway from this initial evaluation of you.

☑ Always know your audience.

☑ Audiovisual aids can improve your presentation substantially.

☑ Connecting or "bridging" statements provide a natural transition from the power opener to the main part of your talk.

☑ There are four guidelines to remember about the bridging concept:

1. Meet your introducer before your presentation.
2. Know the content of the introduction in advance.
3. Bridge opening remarks into the introduction.
4. Bridge closing remarks back to the introduction.

☑ When no formal introduction will be given, bridge your talk to a current event.

☑ It's often very effective to use some kind of attention-grabbing statement as your bridging device.

CHAPTER 3

The Main Body:
Guidelines for Preparing
Your Business Presentation

This chapter explores the heart of your presentation: the main body. During this part of your talk, you highlight for the audience the major points of your presentation, offering supporting statements and examples that help to "sell" your theme.

You'll learn how to prepare the main body of your talk using a simple outline format that helps you pinpoint the major topics to be discussed. As a special feature, checklists are provided for five "typical" business presentations, offering suggestions on what to write for:

- An Annual Divisional Review
- A Marketing Presentation
- A New Sales Plan
- Establishing a Sales Training Department
- Employing an Outside Marketing Consulting Firm

Much of the information offered in the checklists can be easily adapted to a number of business topics. In short, this chapter offers the fundamental guidelines you need when preparing your own business presentation.

Selling the Primary Theme of Your Talk

With the completion of both the power opener and connector, your presentation is now ready to progress into the *main body* of the talk. This is a crucial phase, since you are now concentrating on building a desire within your audience, namely the need to know more about what is being presented. In essence, the main body is a compilation of the key points you wish to present. Note the multiple purposes it serves:

- It provides a smooth entry into the main reason for your talk, offering (where appropriate) pertinent examples, facts, and figures.
- It reinforces your viewpoint to the audience with emphasis on key points.
- It demonstrates a clear rationale for the presentation itself by working through the communication process in a clear, orderly fashion.

Depending upon the type (and complexity) of the business presentation, the *main body* can vary in length from just a few moments to over one hour. To illustrate, let's turn back once more and tune in to an abbreviated cross-section on Sally Field's presentation on the revised appraisal system.

Sample Main Body

"So . . . as you will note, the proposed appraisal form revision will give us a far superior system in the following specific ways:

"For the first time, we have defined performance criteria for each major job classification, with a clear rationale for the rating criteria to be used.

"Second, the appraisal form has been specifically designed to be <u>mutually participative</u>, with the employee being appraised and having the opportunity to both <u>read and react</u> to the supervisor's comments, <u>prior</u> to the formal appraisal session.

"Third, where full agreement on all appraisal factors has <u>not</u> been reached, a nonthreatening <u>exception report</u> can be filed by the employee. In effect, this places the disputed evaluation into a neutral third-party status.

"Next, between each of the formal six-month appraisal periods, specific areas of improvement (and how they will be obtained) will be jointly determined by both the employee and their supervisor.

"Finally, this revised performance appraisal system contains a built-in motivator which everyone is sure to like. For the first time, the appraisal system will <u>tie in directly</u> to the employee's annual compensation review. No more will we have our current 'hit or miss' method of compensation. From here on in, <u>it's performance that will count!</u>"

Here is how Sally's presentation would look when broken down into key summary points and descriptions of visual aids.

SUMMARY POINTS	VISUAL AIDS
3. *Main Body:*	TRANSPARENCY 4
PROPOSED REVISIONS	PROPOSED REVISIONS
Performance Criteria	• Use of performance Criteria
• Defined for each major job classification	• Major job Classifications
• Mutually Participative	• Highly participative
• Exception report to smooth out disagreements	• Exception report
• Areas of improvement to be jointly determined	TRANSPARENCY 5 (PROPOSED REVISIONS CONTINUED)
• New system ties performance directly to Compensation	• Improvement areas
• End of "hit or miss" method	• Performance and compensation
	• A fairer system for all
	• No more "shots in the dark!"

Preparing the Main Body of Your Talk

Now that you've written your opening and connecting link, you are ready to prepare the main body of your talk. In the space provided below, write the main points you wish to highlight. Then add any statements which support or reinforce your main ideas.

Main Heading: _____

Supporting Statements:

- _____
- _____
- _____

Main Heading: _____

Supporting Statements:

- _____
- _____
- _____

Main Heading: _____

Supporting Statements:

- _____
- _____
- _____

Main Heading: _____

Supporting Statements:

- _____
- _____
- _____

Using Sally Field's presentation shown on page 45 as an example, summarize the outline you just prepared onto the following form. Add any visual aids you plan to use.

Speaker Tips:

- Just prior to writing the main body, check your power opener and connector again. This will help in providing good continuity when developing the main body.
- During the main body of the talk, it's especially important to use as much body language as possible, to enhance the positive psychological mood that you are conveying to the audience.
- The main body of your presentation can be made much more effective by the occasional use of pauses ... for hyping audience interest and attention.

SUMMARY POINTS	VISUAL AIDS
3. *Main Body:*	

What to Write: Checklists for Preparing Five Typical Business Presentations

Naturally, every presentation is different, and every company has its own unique problems and opportunities that set it apart from all the rest. It would not be possible to provide a detailed breakdown of material for inclusion to a talk on the annual budget, for example, because so many variables depend on your company's specific circumstances.

Nevertheless, there are certain guidelines that can be offered for preparing "typical" business presentations often encountered. In the next few pages you'll find checklists to help you with the following: an annual divisional review, a new sales plan, a marketing presentation, establishing a sales training department, and employing an outside marketing consulting firm.

Whether or not your presentation is on one of these topics, you'll find the checklists to be helpful aids in compiling and organizing the information you need. Most of the material included in the checklists can be easily adapted to suit your business presentation's own individual needs.

Annual Divisional Review Checklist

Background
How did the division perform last year? Was it financially better or worse than previous years?

How would you classify the division as a whole: stable, volatile, growing or stagnant?

Is this past year's performance a problem or something to be proud of? What do you hope to change for next year?

Sales History and Projections
What is the division's sales performance record? (Consider a three- to five-year period, for example.)

What projections do you have for future sales?

How successful were your advertising efforts this past year?

What are your advertising objectives for next year?

Annual Divisional Review Checklist (*Continued*)

Marketing

What new products are you planning for next year?

Are any further changes planned? If yes, what impact will they have on the division?

Is competition a factor? If yes, how?

Describe any marketing objectives that could have impact on the division next year.

Describe how well the division performed from a marketing standpoint during the past year.

Personnel

Have you lost or gained divisional personnel during the past year? How has this affected employees?

How did salaries and incentive programs fare over the past year? How will they differ next year?

Do you have plans for reorganizing the division next year? How will this affect employees specifically?

New Sales Plan Checklist

Background
What important changes have occurred in the structure of the company, including management or ownership, that have had an impact on the sales force?

How many customers or active accounts were there under the old system?

Are there seasonal or other restrictions that affect selling your product?

Why traditionally do customers buy your product: price, delivery, timing, performance, etc.?

How long was the old sales plan in effect? What prompted your company to devise a new sales plan? (Was the old system unfair or financially insufficient? Be as specific as possible.)

What were the major accomplishments achieved under the old system?

New Sales Plan Checklist (*Continued*)

The New Sales Plan
When is the new plan scheduled to become effective? (State any reasons for a delay, training programs that may need to be initiated, etc.)

Highlight the key features and benefits of the new plan.

Special Sales Considerations
How will the new sales plan affect the following:

New accounts? _____
_____

Sales territories? _____
_____

Compensation to sales reps? _____
_____

Salaries versus commissions? _____
_____

Reimbursements for expenses? _____
_____

Paper work? _____

Communication between field and
in-house staff? _____
_____

Other: _____
_____

Marketing Presentation Checklist

Background
Describe the market. Include history, size, trends, and your product's position in the market.

Is the market changing? Compare today's market with the one five years ago. Then compare today's market with the market you envision five years in the future.

Describe your three primary competitors, their products, and their marketing strategies.

Competitor 1: _____
Product: _____
Marketing strategy: _____
Strengths: _____
Weaknesses: _____

Competitor 2: _____
Product: _____
Marketing strategy: _____
Strengths: _____
Weaknesses: _____

Competitor 3: _____
Product: _____
Marketing strategy: _____
Strengths: _____
Weaknesses: _____

Marketing Presentation Checklist (*Continued*)

Special Marketing Considerations
You may also wish to consider some or all of the following market aspects when preparing your presentation.

☐ Market share

☐ Pricing objectives

☐ Channels of distribution

☐ Personnel requirements

☐ Customer-client relationships

☐ Advertising and sales promotion

☐ Sales projections
    — by region or territory
    — for all product lines

☐ Budget restrictions or allowances

☐ Any proposed government regulations that could affect your marketing strategy

☐ Marketing plan, annual report, newsletter, or other material furnished by your company which may be helpful in obtaining information

Sales Training Department Checklist

Background

What significant changes have occurred in the industry to make the environment much more competitive for our projects?

Based upon current feedback from company interviewers, describe several characteristics/traits of the "new-breed" college graduate applying for a sales position in our industry.

What factors in the past has caused your organization *not* to create formalized sales training department?

Compare those factors with the significant industry changes that have now occurred, the expectations of the "new breed" . . . and determine whether it is now feasible to establish formalized sales training.

Industry Changes	"New-Breed" Expectations	Previous Factors Of No Training	Revised Factors
_____	_____	_____	_____
_____	_____	_____	_____
_____	_____	_____	_____
_____	_____	_____	_____
_____	_____	_____	_____

Objectives

Describe what should be accomplished by formalized sales training:

- Within the first year _____
- Second year _____
- Years 3 to 5 _____

Sales Training Department Checklist (*Continued*)

Resources
How many people will it take to staff this department?
List each by job function

For each major position in the department, can you recruit from "inside the organization" (or, do you have to advertise)?

Programs
To support key objectives, list all courses planned for the first 12 months, costs assigned to each and general time-frame involved for completion.

Course	(Cost) Developed In-House	(Cost) Developed By Consultant	Time-Frame For Completion	Special Factors (If any)

Space Requirements
How much space will be needed to house this new department?

Is it now available, or will it have to be secured from somewhere else?

What is the cost of this space?

Timetable
Assuming approval is forthcoming, how quickly can the new sales training department begin functioning?

Results Measurement
How will results be measured? (Performance vs. Expectations)

First Year:

Second Year:

Years 3 to 5:

Outside Marketing Consulting Firm Checklist

Background
What is the current capability of our Market Research Department? _____

Existing strengths of this group: _____
_____

Areas where additional expertise are required: _____
_____

Opportunity cost factors involved in not receiving full amount of marketing research required for next
calendar year: _____
_____

Research Required
List all marketing research needed for next calendar year, include the budget allocation and check
whether or not it can be supplied by your existing department.

Type	Budget Allocation	Can Be Supplied-in-House	Need Outside Consulting Firm
Existing Line			
_____	_____	_____	_____
_____	_____	_____	_____
_____	_____	_____	_____
New Products			
_____	_____	_____	_____
_____	_____	_____	_____
_____	_____	_____	_____
Advertising Research			
_____	_____	_____	_____
_____	_____	_____	_____
_____	_____	_____	_____
Consumer Research			
_____	_____	_____	_____
_____	_____	_____	_____
_____	_____	_____	_____
Other Research			
_____	_____	_____	_____
_____	_____	_____	_____
_____	_____	_____	_____

Outside Marketing Consulting Firm Checklist (*Continued*)

Consultants

List all consulting firms having expertise in those research areas where outside assistance is desired.

Name/Address	Key Contact	Telephone	Field of Specialization
1. _____	_____	_____	_____
2. _____	_____	_____	_____
3. _____	_____	_____	_____
4. _____	_____	_____	_____
5. _____	_____	_____	_____

For each consultant being interviewed, list selection criteria to be used:

1. Reputation
2. Expertise
3. Quality of presentation made to your group
4. Reference checks
5. Fees/charge
6. Type of contract
7. _____
8. _____
9. _____
10. _____

Selection Committee

List those people who should be involved in each presentation and whether or not they have a vote in the final selection of the consultant to be employed.

Name	Should Have Vote In Final Selection	No Vote In Final Selection
1. _____	_____	_____
2. _____	_____	_____
3. _____	_____	_____
4. _____	_____	_____

Time Frames

Determine in advance the feasible deadlines involved for each outside research project.

Project	Initial Consultant Visit	Time Frame for Subsequent Visits	Review of Proposal	Final Selection
1. _____	_____	_____	_____	_____
2. _____	_____	_____	_____	_____
3. _____	_____	_____	_____	_____
4. _____	_____	_____	_____	_____
5. _____	_____	_____	_____	_____

Speaker Tips:

Annual Divisional Review

- For this category of presentation, remember to be especially prepared for a multitude of questions both during and after the talk.
- Regarding audiovisual, heavy use of charts and graphs (in color) will enhance the presentation.

New Sales Plan

- When presenting the new sales plan, always take into account the normal "resistance to change." Accordingly, polish-up the WIFMs and make frequent use of benefit statements which show the advantages of implementing the new plan.
- Make especially certain to illustrate how much the new plan will cost, versus the existing one. If the new plan costs substantially more, make sure that the rationale for this is reflected in the main body of the talk.

Marketing Presentation

- During the marketing presentation, try for heavy use of audiovisual support (35 mm slides, overhead transparencies in color, etc.). This in effect, will help "sell" the overall presentation. Avoid the color red, and concentrate on blues, yellows and greens (proven to be more appealing to the eye, in contrast to red, which is a "caution" color).
- Make certain that you have as many facts and figures as possible on your competitors. Experience has shown that this is usually the weakest area of the presentation.

Sales Training Department

- Caution
  - Any presentation on the creation of a sales training department has to be handled with care. Remember that this is a pure expense item (with no clear revenue stream attached). Hence, rationale for same must be highly convincing. Accordingly:
  - Be prepared for many questions.
  - Carefully develop the Power-Opener for maximum effectiveness
  - In main body of talk, stress benefits of proposal.
  - Try for the strongest closing possible, with a restatement of benefits, and the ending built around a highly positive note.
- If you are not an authority on sales training, you may want to have a "subject matter expert" available to assist you as questions arise.

Speaker Tips (continued):

Outside Consulting Firm

- Be aware that there are usually strong opinions (both pro and con) regarding the use of outside consulting firms. If possible, try to determine how many favorable "decision-influencers" will be in your audience ... since you may have to count on them for support.
- Make certain that you have included all marketing research projects that need to be carried out for the time period in question (usually a calendar year) and specifically identify those projects which are not feasible to do "in-house". This will lend reinforcement to your proposals to employ an outside firm.
- Remember to keep the general tone of the presentation "low-keyed", highly professional, and avoid the use of humor. Strong WIFMs liberally sprinkled throughout the talk will be a definite plus.

Chapter Summary

You have now successfully finished the study of the main body together with the supporting guidelines involved. You've reviewed a sample of the main body for an actual presentation, and critiqued checklists for preparing five typical business talks.

Now you are ready to start work on the power close . . . that section of the business presentation that can strongly affect the degree of success you obtain at the end of the talk. If you have already done a reasonably good job with the power opener, connectors, and main body, an effective power close can almost guarantee you a winning presentation.

Memory Joggers

☑ The main body is a compilation of the key points you wish to present. It serves multiple purposes, in that:

— It provides a smooth entry into the main reason your talk, offering (where appropriate) pertinent examples, facts and figures

— It reinforces your viewpoint to the audience with emphasis on key points

— It demonstrates a clear rationale for the presentation, by working through the communication process in a clear, orderly manner

☑ Before writing the main body, recheck the power opener and connector. Make certain that there is a good continuity flow from one segment to the other

☑ During your actual talk, the main body can be greatly enhanced by the use of both appropriate body language and occasional use of pauses for effect

☑ Remember that the main body provides the most fertile field for audience questions. When preparing the talk, make a special point in anticipating all possible questions that could arise

☑ Keep in mind that it is in the main body section where you will either convince (or persuade) the audience to your point of view or lose them. Further, this portion of your presentation (if done effectively) will greatly aid in the power close.

CHAPTER 4

Power Closes: How to Gain the Commitment of Your Audience

This chapter focuses on the key aspect of how to close your talk in the most effective manner. Done properly, it will secure audience commitment to the objective the talk was developed for.

You will learn the simplified three-step sequence which can turn an ordinary end of a presentation into one that the audience will remember, and pave the way for commitment for all those who heard the presentation.

As a special aid in developing your own power closes, examples of this technique will be given for a power close based on:

- shock value
- a real-world situation
- a current event
- a well-known figure
- an enigma

Forms and checklists are also provided to allow you to transfer this new skill directly to your next talk.

How the Applied Closing Technique Works

By the time you reach your closing, you should have received some form of commitment from the audience, or an indication that your message has been not only heard, but accepted. As a result, your audience should now be:

- informed of a particular situation (and in a position to do something about it)
- persuaded by your talk to take some form of action
- reinforced by a current attitude (whether positive or negative)
- stimulated to enter into type of behavior change
- motivated to take or develop a new course of action

Speaker Tips:

A business presentation closely parallels the same objectives and progressions as a sales call. In both cases, the speaker (or the salesperson) attempts to secure some type of commitment from the people being addressed.

Most professional speakers rely on the time-tested applied closing technique to help them "sell" their presentation (see figure 4-1). There are three steps involved:

1. Rephrasing (or partially rephrasing) of key points
2. Power close summary
3. Use of benefit statement where applicable

Let's take a closer look at each of the three steps involved.

Step 1: Rephrasing of Key Points

To help build the proper power close, the speaker needs to reinforce positively the main elements of the presentation—with special highlighting of the key points that each person in the audience should remember after the presentation has concluded.

Using audiovisual aids during rephrasing can be extremely effective; for example, displaying your summary points on 35mm slides, overhead transparencies, or flipcharts.

To illustrate the importance of rephrasing (or partial rephrasing), let's turn to the power close phase on the proposed revision of Sally Field's talk on the new performance appraisal system.

APPLIED CLOSING TECHNIQUE

Rephrasing
(or partially paraphrasing)
of key points

Power close summary

Use of benefit statement
(where applicable)

FIGURE 4-1
Applied Closing Techniques

Sample rephrasing technique

Here, Sally has just turned to a new page on the flipchart and has resumed her presentation.

"As you can all see from this summary page, there are numerous benefits in implementing our proposed employee performance appraisal plan. Although we haven't listed <u>every</u> single advantage that's involved, the key benefits featured are:

- *The system supplies every manager (and supervisor) with a more <u>effective performance measurement tool</u> and a built-in mechanism for more effective employee <u>coaching</u> where required.*
- *It is perceived as a <u>much fairer system</u> than the current one, the proposed system should provide a definite <u>boost to employee morale</u>.*
- *We now will have a <u>direct link between specific performance</u> and the annual <u>compensation</u> review.*
- *The revised system not only provides for continuity on a six-month basis, but also supplies an easy-to-use <u>coaching tool</u> to improve employee performance <u>between</u> formal appraisal periods.*
- *The new system is highly flexible, such that <u>performance criteria can be modified</u> where necessary—and <u>mutually participative</u> with both supervisor and employee working closely together for the common good."*

Step 2: The Power Close Summary

With the completion of the rephrasing, the speaker is now ready to highlight the *power close summary. The importance of this step cannot be overemphasized.* If it is done correctly, at the conclusion of the presentation, the audience will probably remember both the *rephrasing of key points* and the *power close summary*, and perhaps very little of the presentation's other parts. Once again, here's an illustration of this from Sally's presentation.

Sample power close summary

"Apparently, the amount of time and effort that went into the revised performance appraisal system is now ready to pay-off. All that is required to implement it, is a three-quarter affirmative majority vote from the management committee. Once approved, the system should be fully operational within three to four weeks."

Step 3: Use of Benefit Statement

Let's see how Sally Field connects her power close summary with a final benefit statement that triggers an action request.

Sample use of a benefit statement

"By approving the plan now, we are assured of implementing one of the finest performance appraisal systems available today and having it completely installed before the end of the month. It's an opportunity that none of us can afford to miss!"

Tips for Using Power Closes

Keep in mind that the main objective of the power close is to guide the audience to some form of action, and it does so by *developing audience commitment*.

To strengthen your power close, keep the following tips in mind:

1. *Always bridge the power close from the main body.* You have already deepened audience desire and involvement with the main body—now capitalize on it with an effective connector.
2. *Build your power close around something the audience will easily relate to.* Refer to a current event, a real world situation, etc. and tie that into the close.
3. *Increase use of nonverbal communication aids.* Gesture with hands, shift position of body, use a pointer (where appropriate) walk in front of the podium or use any other type of non-verbal signal to emphasize the close.
4. *Use your voice to its best advantage.* You can:
   - Increase (or decrease) your rate of speech
   - Raise (or lower) your sound level
   - Pause for effect . . . then begin speaking again

Five Sample Power Close Techniques

Here are five power close examples.

1. Power Close Based on Shock Value

"Now, as we have just seen from the last slide, unless we received an immediate increase in our whole-blood supply, 150 patients a day will be in immediate danger. Translated another way, it could mean:

- *a 50 percent increase in patient deaths due to lack of blood for transfusions*
- *postponement of the majority of critically needed major operations*
- *having the majority of our hospitals turning away most newly requested patient admissions*

". . . the rest is up to you. In order to avert this kind of disaster scenario, I'm requesting everyone in this audience to sign up for the company blood drive that begins this afternoon in the cafeteria at 4:00 PM. Just pick up the slips by the main exit door upon leaving, complete the requested information, and hand it to your supervisor by noon today.

"And, remember, the life you save, may be your own . . ."

2. Power Close Based on a Real-World Situation

Note: Due to the frequency with which this situation can be used, two power close examples are given.

Example 1

"Based on our latest readings of the revised tax law, many of the previously allowed tax-shelters are no longer valid. Unless many of you in this room begin to change your retirement strategy planning, you will experience fewer benefits at age 65 due to:

- *weakening of the IRA structure*
- *reduction of contributions in 401 K*
- *higher taxing of working spouses*

"However, you can begin to change all of these grim statistics by enrolling in our new staff incentive compensation plan. Instead of taking your guaranteed two to four percent cash bonus at the end of each year, we recommend that you re-invest that amount with us, and the company will match that corresponding number and place the entire amount in a tax-deferred fund until your retirement. In other words, if you received at four percent bonus in December, it would be considered income, and you would be taxed accordingly. However, by reinvesting it with us you would earn tax-free dollars on eight percent.

"To take advantage of this, merely sign the authorization cards now being distributed. By acting now, you are guaranteeing a higher level of income for yourself upon retirement from this company.

"Not a bad trade-off at all! We urge you to be included in this new company benefit immediately!"

Example 2

"Based on these latest facts and figures, the reality of the situation can be summed up this way. Within the next six months, our company will either survive, or be forced to shut its doors and lay off the entire work force.

"To remain solvent, starting next month, and continuing for the next twelve months (at a minimum), we must find a way to:

- *increase sales by 10 to 15 percent*
- *reduce our overhead costs by a minimum of 20 percent*
- *increase line productivity by 25 percent*

"As each of you leaves this room and returns to your respective units, your manager will outline those specific steps required from your work unit to help us accomplish our goal.

"I'm counting on each of you. Good luck . . . and let's go!"

3. A Power Close Based on a Current Event

"It should be clear now, that unless we take immediate steps to reduce our budget deficit, we will be heading for a full-blown recession.

"As a result, all of us in this room could then look forward to a loss of jobs, a rising unemployment rate, a severe housing slump, and a continued weakness in our dollar abroad. Coupled with this dismal scene, would be the flight of foreign capital from the United States . . . which would only compound our problems even further.

"The only way to stop this madness, is to make your voice loud and clear to congress; that we demand a balanced budget to restore our fiscal integrity . . . before its too late!

"By sending a telegram to the address listed on the flipchart, we just might start reversing this alarming trend towards doomsday.

"And then, maybe, we can all sleep a little better tonight!"

4. Power Close Based on a Well-Known Figure

"So, as we have witnessed during the past half hour, the situation is very bleak.

- *Our sales are down, while the industry goes up.*
- *Net revenue is down by an alarming 5 percent.*

"Well, as I said earlier in this talk, our president is a fighter, and so am I. So, in addition to 'rolling up my sleeves' to turn this company around, I expect everyone in this room to do the same.

"The 'buckaroo' stops with me, but by working together as a team nobody can beat us. Both my grandfather and father pulled this company through hard times, and I intend to do the same . . ."

5. Power Close Based on an Enigma

"Now, the facts and figures are quite clear.

- *Forty percent of the people in this room are over 35 years old.*
- *Statistically, at least half of this group are probably approaching a high-risk category due to inflated cholesterol levels, smoking and insufficient daily exercise.*
- *Therefore, there is a good chance that based on this trend, at least 4 people in this room today, will be dead within the next 8 to 10 years!*

"Shocking? You bet! But the answer is equally clear . . . enrollment in the new corporate fitness program—which allows each of you one full hour each day of supervised exercise. This can be arranged to be done during your lunch hour, or (if more convenient) before the start of work.

"And, since the company contributes approximately 70 percent of the total cost, your outlay is only one dollar per day!

"Start a program to begin prolonging your life today . . . take the first step and enroll before leaving this room!"

Speaker Tips:

- Rephrase key points early in the close.
- Make certain summary is as concise as possible.
- Always close your talk with a benefit statement (or WIFM) wherever possible.
- Never lose eye contact with audience during the close!

Creating Your Own Power Close

Let's use Sally Field's presentation as an example of how to summarize a closing. Now based on the material already covered in your power opener, connector, and main body, prepare your own power close in the space provided on page 69.

SUMMARY POINTS	VISUAL AIDS
4. Power Close:	TRANSPARENCY 6: BENEFITS OF PROPOSED SYSTEM • Simpler, easier to implement • Performance measurement • More effective coaching • Fairer system than before
BENEFITS OF REVISED SYSTEM • More effective performance measurement • Much fairer system • Definite morale booster • Provides direct link between performance and compensation	TRANSPARENCY 7: BENEFITS (cont'd) • Will help morale • Links performance and compensation • Highly participative
WHAT'S NOW REQUIRED • ¾ affirmative majority vote • System can be operating within a month	TRANSPARENCY 8: NEED TO DO • Vote yes as a committee • ¾ majority required • Can install in next 4 weeks
SUMMARY • We need it • It's here • Let's move on it!	TRANSPARENCY 9: SUMMARY • Move quickly, or we miss the chance

SUMMARY POINTS	VISUAL AIDS
4. *Power Close:*	

Chapter Summary

With the completion of this chapter, you have learned how to create and use a power close to successfully end a business presentation.

You have surfaced the key steps needed to create a power close, and for the sake of continuity, used power closes based on the same types of situations developed in Chapter 2 (Power Openers). These were closes built around

- shock value
- a real world situation

- a current event
- a well known personality
- an enigma

And, to reinforce the real world transfer of this skill to your next talk, we again presented an example of Sally Field's talk on the new performance appraisal system as written on the key point summarizer.

At this juncture, you're ready to tackle the next chapter which deals with the handling of audience questions . . . both when they are raised naturally from the group, and when none are forthcoming (but should be).

Memory Joggers

☑ There are three steps involved in the closing techniques:

1. Rephrasing of key points
2. Power close summary
3. Use of benefit statement

☑ Using audiovisual aids during rephrasing stage can be very effective.

☑ An effective power close builds on the desire (created by the main body) and commits the audience to some type of action.

☑ For maximum effect, always bridge the power close from the main body.

☑ Try to develop power closes around something the audience will quickly relate to. For example:

1. A close based on shock value
2. Power close built around a real-world situation
3. One based on a current event
4. A power close centered around a well-known figure
5. One based on a enigma

☑ Always use non-verbal communication aids during the close.

☑ A really powerful close usually contains a pause . . . to heighten interest and suspense.

CHAPTER 5

How to Handle
Audience Questions

This chapter explores the fifth and final element of a successful business presentation: anticipating audience questions and learning how to answer them properly.

You'll find key strategies for handling questions from the audience and three ways to "break the ice" when you meet with a nonresponsive group. In addition, you'll see why writing anticipated questions in advance on index cards can prove an invaluable aid in your preplanning strategy.

How to Anticipate Questions or Objections

In order to give a successful presentation, it is essential that every conceivable type of question or objection that might be raised by the audience is anticipated in *advance* of the presentation.

Preplanning Strategy

- List all possible questions you think might be asked by the audience and corresponding answers which can be used.
- Put the questions and answers on index cards (an example is shown in Figure 5-1). Remember when using index cards, that it is usually best to place one question and answer per card.
- Review each question and answer with an associate prior to the talk.
- Be flexible; liberally add any additional questions and answers to the list.

- Review the list one more time; then decide whether it would be more appropriate to handle questions as they arise during the talk, or to request that the audience hold all comments until the end of your talk. (Note: There is no right or wrong answer here. Both approaches work equally well).

TITLE OF TALK: *Proposal for Increased Productivity*

DATE TO BE GIVEN: 1/4/88

ANTICIPATED QUESTION: *"A planned reduction of 20% in our overtime expense sounds like a fine idea—but just how do you intend doing this? In my opinion, it's far easier said than done!"*

PLANNED RESPONSE: *"Can be done in three steps:*

1. Analysis of peak workloads (where heaviest overtime occurs) during past 3 months.

2. Heavier use of part-time temps to fill unexpected demand.

3. More effective scheduling of work force through better planning of first two steps."

FIGURE 5-1:
Anticipated Questions/Response Form

At Conclusion of Presentation

- Solicit questions from the audience, but always let the group know if there are any kind of constraints or time limitations.
- As a courtesy to the audience, if a time constraint arises during questioning, specify how many additional questions you can answer before time runs out.
- If time does run out before all questions are answered, try to remain after the presentation has formally concluded and speak individually to people who may still have questions.

The Ice-Breakers: What to Do When No Questions Are Asked

Sometimes, despite the best of planning on your part, you may find yourself facing an audience that offers no reaction to your talk, yet you feel certain the group has opinions that should be shared. The skill required is to get someone in the audience to be the first to "break the ice" and ask a question. Here are three simple strategies.

Ice-Breaker I: The Open-Ended Question

With this method, you casually state an open question that members of the audience are sure to have an opinion on, wait briefly for a response, and then answer it yourself. By offering your opinion, you also will invite reaction from your audience.

> *Example:*
> *"Guess that about sums up my point of view on the new bonus proposal. We have allotted about fifteen minutes to now answer any questions or concerns you may have. So . . . any questions?" (silence!) . . .*
> *"Well, okay . . . while you are considering questions on how this will affect both you and your departments, here's a point that I'm asked to clarify everywhere this talk is given! This concerns itself with how the union rank and file are going to react to this new incentive system. Well, in my opinion. . ."*

Ice Breaker II: Motivate Audience Response

Ask the same type of general question, then motivate audience interest through an actual involvement step . . . such as a voice vote, show of hands, etc.

> *Example (using the same lead-in question as before):*
> *"Guess that about sums up my point of view on the new bonus proposal. We have allotted about fifteen minutes to now answer any questions or concerns you may have. So . . . any questions?" (silence!) . . .*
> *"Well, I don't hear any questions, but I bet you all have very strong opinions either way. For example, everyone in this room who feels that the bonus proposal doesn't go far enough in incentive compensation, raise your hand."*

Ice-Breaker III: Secure an Active Response

Follow the same procedure as Ice-Breaker II, but secure involvement with a participant. Using firm eye contact, ask a general question from someone in the audience who has been an active listener (as evidenced by their verbal and/or non-verbal language during your presentation).

> *Example (using the same lead-in question as before):*
> *"Well, I don't hear any questions, but I know some of you have definite feelings both pro and con on the bonus proposal. Let's see . . . Herb, you appeared both pleased and concerned during my presentation. How about sharing those feelings with us."*

The "Paraphrase" Strategy

The cardinal rule in answering any audience question is to *paraphrase* (either completely or partially) before responding directly to the question itself. This method gives the speaker an immediate dual advantage:

1. It enables everyone in the audience to understand fully what has been asked, thus avoiding any potential type of confusion or misunderstanding on anyone's part.
2. By paraphrasing (or partially paraphrasing), the speaker is automatically given a few extra seconds to plan for the answer).

Now, here's a technique rarely found in text or workbooks. It applies to situations where you (the speaker) *have forgotten what was asked*, or *are not absolutely certain of the correct answer*.

Regarding the latter situation, it's perfectly acceptable for a speaker (who is not sure of an answer) to tell the participant that the question will be researched and an answer forthcoming shortly. However, there *will be* times when the answer is actually known, but the speaker does require a few seconds to get a "mental fix" on what was just spoken. In situations like this, either of the following two techniques can be used:

Technique 1: Rephrase Question

After the question has been asked, request person to "Please rephrase the question so that it will be clear to everyone in the room."

Example:
"Thanks for the question. However, since we are in such a large room, I wonder if you could rephrase the question to make sure everyone has heard it."

Note: Even though only a few seconds are involved in the repeating of the question, it is usually enough time for the speaker to consider the appropriate answer.

Technique 2: Repeat Question

This skill comes into play when (a) the speaker needs additional time to respond, or (b) the benefit of group thinking would be highly beneficial before the official response from the speaker.

Example:
"The question has just been asked regarding the rationale for hiring additional temporary personnel in lieu of giving our existing staff the overtime pay. I realize that there are strong opinions on this either way; so before giving my answer, I'm curious as to how the majority of you feel. Who would like to respond to this?"

Caution: Both techniques will allow you a few moments before a response has to be given. However, if there is an occasion where you simply do not know the answer, *never* try to trick the audience by avoiding the question. In the final analysis, the talk will suffer, the speaker's credibility will have been diminished, and in the end, the speaker becomes the real loser.

Why You Should Consider Every Question as an Opportunity

Regardless of the type of business presentation, the speaker should always consider each question as an *opportunity* to reinforce the talk.

One obvious advantage is that the questions themselves are clear proof that the audience is interested and involved with your talk (giving you an opportunity to continue building and strengthening the talk.

Finally, never lose patience with an audience that tosses a seemingly heavy flow of questions at you. Unless you were terribly vague (hence, the high degree of questions), these audience requests for clarification usually represent a tribute to the degree of interest stirred up by your presentation.

Typical Audience Questions for Five Types of Presentations

As a guide to possible questions you may be asked at the conclusion of your talk, here are typical audience queries for the five sample business presentations listed in chapter three. You should not consider these questions as being all-inclusive to each topic, but merely a guide to stimulate building your own list for the next talk given. To encourage this, try adding a few questions of your own in the blank space provided.

Speaker Tips:

Every business presentation made will be different from the previous one and from the next. Depending on the nature of the presentation, how the "message" is conveyed by the speaker and the audience, one of the following scenarios will likely take place.

- Mild audience interest: only a few interspersed, scattered grouping of questions.
- Moderate audience attention: reasonable interplay of questions and answers from assembled group of participants and speaker.
- Lively audience interest/attention: both during and after talk, participants maintain high level of awareness of heavily probed speaker with relevant questions.

Annual Divisional Review: Sample Audience Questions

1. You listed only divisional performance last year. How does it look compared to the past three years?

2. Personally, I think you are being too optimistic in your growth forecast, especially for next year. Please give me your rationale for this.

3. How do we compare in sales with our three major competitors?

4. Seems to me that you have ignored economic factors in your sales projection. What if a recession comes next year? Have you considered that?

5. Frankly, I don't see enough in next year's budget for market research. How did you arrive at that number?

6. Granted, we had a great track record this year . . . but where are the new products for next year . . . to sustain our target of 15 percent annual growth?

7. Perhaps I've misunderstood, but I still don't think that you have clearly defined our marketing objectives for next year. Would you clarify this for me, please?

8. Very little was said about human resources and it's impact on our productivity. Care to comment?

9. I liked your presentation, but you have completely ignored the fact that we have twice the employee turnover as any of our competitors. Why is that?

10. Let's go back for a moment to this year's gross margin on overseas sales. I'm not sure how you arrived at this percentage.

11.

12.

13.

New Sales Plan: Sample Audience Questions

1. Why aren't we implementing the new sales plan immediately? Seems rather silly to wait until the next quarter to start it.

2. I like the main concept of the plan, but feel that you have not focused enough attention on sales achievement versus compensation. What are your thoughts on this?

3. What you say makes sense, but I still feel that the current plan more than meets our needs. Have you considered this in your planning?

4. Frankly, the new sales plan just seems like a lot more paperwork to me, and, how can you justify that?

5. Can we go over the section on realignment of territories? Personally, I think it favors the southern areas at the expense of the western region.

6. Why haven't you mentioned anything about the advertising support necessary to implement this new sales plan . . . or am I missing the point?

7. I like the way you have presented this, but think that you are overly optimistic about increasing our new accounts by 20 percent as a result. Care to explain?

8. The plan looks terrific. Do you plan to also present this to our middle management team? If so, how soon can you do it?

9. I'm really concerned about the pricing strategy in the plan. I think you are way off the mark. *Your* thoughts?

10.

11.

12.

13.

Marketing Presentation: Sample Audience Questions

1. Would you mind elaborating on our projected market share for the next two years? Personally, I think you are being far too conservative.

2. Your presentation was quite good, however, I wish you would amplify on how the market is rapidly changing for our products. Would you mind?

3. Where in your presentation was the profile of our three biggest competitors? I heard we are losing ground to each of them almost every month! What is your position on this?

4. I still believe that your sales projections for next year are at least 40 percent higher than can be expected. How did you arrive at this number?

5. What is the rationale for establishing next year's pricing objectives?

6. Why are you so confident that consumer spending will go up by 15 percent for next year? Who are your sources of information?

7. Frankly, you have not convinced me about the need for budget restrictions during the next six months. Besides, what will the union say?

8. Nice presentation, but you omitted any reference to sales promotion. Was this done deliberately?

9. What's the size of our total market? In your opinion, is this market expanding or shrinking?

10. Somehow, you have consistently downplayed the negative effect of state taxation on our cost of goods sold. Care to explain?

11.

12.

13.

Creation of a Sales Training Department: Sample Audience Questions

1. You raise many valid points, but I still think that the results of sales training can never be measured, so how can you state that we need it?

2. So . . . where do we get the person to manage this new department? Certainly, there is no one internally who could fill this position.

3. Regarding expenses for the first year, why do you include the cost of outside consultants? Why can't our own staff do the work?

4. Why haven't you covered the space requirements of this new department? And where do you plan to locate them?

5. Why do we have to create a whole new department at all? How about hiring an outside consultant only when needed?

6. We've never had a sales training department, and our sales go up at least 10 percent every year. How do you explain that?

7. I'm still confused as to how much this proposed department will really cost. Would you mind going over the numbers once more?

8. Do you know what each of our competitors does in the way of formalized sales training?

9. I'm really excited about your plan. How fast can we move on this?

10. Unless you can convince me otherwise, I feel that we should defer this plan for at least one year—what do you say about that?

11.

12.

13.

Feasibility of Hiring an Outside Marketing Consultant Firm: Sample Audience Questions

1. While I agree with the need for outside expertise, I'm not sure your list of recommended consultants is complete. Who compiled it?

2. Once we agree on the firms to be interviewed, who will do the interviewing . . . and most importantly, the final selection?

3. Frankly, I think you have terribly underestimated our own market research department. Why can't these people handle the new jobs?

4. Are you certain as to the *extent* of market research required for next year? How did you arrive at these figures?

5. What type of contract has to be signed? What if after six months we decide they are not satisfactory?

6. Have you considered the confidentiality aspect when using outside consultants? How do we protect ourselves?

7. I believe that the selection criteria you just outlined is heavily biased towards the "ivy-league" firms. What's your view on that?

8. This firm has never employed outside marketing consultants before, and I still don't see why we need them now.

9. I like your presentation. When can we start interviewing these firms?

10. Are you certain that none of the firms you listed now works for our competitors? How can you prove that to me?

11.

12.

13.

Preparing Your Own List of Anticipated Questions

Now let's focus on a real-world situation, and return once more to the presentation on the revised performance appraisal system.

After Sally completed the power opener, connecting links, main body and power close, she would, in effect have the complete structure of the talk. By knowing her audience in advance (their WIFMs and expectations) and reflecting on this, she could reasonably anticipate most audience questions. Thereby formulating appropriate responses *in advance* of the talk. As a reality check, we (where possible) would have one of her peers review her talk in advance and supply additional possible audience questions.

To illustrate, here are two examples of audience questions that Sally anticipated together with her planned response.

Possible Audience Questions	Appropriate Responses
1. The proposed plan looks okay, but why must we vote on it now? How about holding off on a decision until we meet again in three weeks?	We have all agreed to the necessity of having the new system operational within the next 3 to 4 weeks. In order to do that, we need your decision today. If any of the facts are still unclear, I'll be happy to review them with you now.
2. Are you certain that our key supervisors will accept a new plan?	Yes. Six of our key supervisors were represented on the steering committee and are 100% in agreement that the new plan is excellent.

Now you're ready for the final step: anticipating the questions you may be asked by your audience. Fill in the main questions you think may be asked in the space provided on the following page, as well as your appropriate response.

	Possible Audience Questions	Appropriate Responses
1.		
2.		
3.		
4.		
5.		

Chapter Summary

You have now successfully finished the section on how to handle audience questions. In doing so, you have learned the preplanning strategy for fielding questions or objections, the three types of "ice-breaker" strategies for countering when no queries are forthcoming (i.e., the open-ended question, that motivates audience response and securing an active response), the "paraphrase" technique of answering every question raised and why you should consider every question as an opportunity.

For real-world transfer of skills, you reviewed typical audience questions for the five sample business presentations listed in chapter three:

- The Annual Divisional Review
- New Sales Plan
- Marketing Presentation
- Creation of a Sales Training Department
- Feasibility of Hiring an Outside Marketing Consulting Firm

You are now in a position to "pull it all together" via the next chapter on the key point summarizer; your practical guide for preparing a broad array of business presentations.

Memory Joggers

☑ Every conceivable type of question or objection that could be raised by the audience must be anticipated in advance of the presentation.

☑ Every question should be considered an opportunity by the speaker.

☑ Index cards are helpful for jotting down and remembering responses to typical questions you expect will be asked.

☑ There are three "ice-breaker" strategies you can use to help encourage the audience to ask questions:

- Ask an open-ended question
- Take the open-ended question a step farther by movtivating your audience to respond.
- Take the open-ended question still further by trying to secure an active response.

☑ Paraphrasing offers a twofold benefit:

1. It helps avoid confusion by enabling everyone in the audience to better understand and/or hear the question that was asked.
2. It allows the speaker a few more seconds to plan his or her answer.

The Key Point Summarizer: Your Guide for Preparing All Types of Business Presentations

In chapters 2 through 5 you followed a sequential process for developing your presentation: (1) create a power opener, (2) use connecting statements or "links" to bridge into (3) the main body, (4) finish with a strong power close, and (5) anticipate audience questions. Now you're ready to combine and condense this information onto one form—the *Key Point Summarizer*.

The key point summarizer is designed to help you turn any type of business presentation into a professional talk. A filled-in sample of the summarizer is shown later in this chapter.

How To Complete the Key Point Summarizer

The summarizer begins with the required base information that you must consider before developing your talk. Within this section you need to determine:

- the title of your presentation
- the date it is to be presented

- an appropriate length of time for your talk
- whether you will be formally or informally introduced
- the room size and anticipated number of people in audience
- whether or not you are known to the audience (which could affect the structure and tone of the presentation)
- the type and number of audiovisual aids to be used in support of the presentation

KEY POINT SUMMARIZER

TITLE OF PRESENTATION: _____
DATE GIVEN: _____
ANTICIPATED DURATION: _____
FORMAL INTRODUCTION: ___ YES ___ NO   INFORMAL INTRODUCTION: ___ YES ___ NO
ROOM DIMENSIONS: _____   AUDIENCE SIZE: _____
FAMILIAR WITH AUDIENCE? ___ YES ___ NO
TYPE OF AUDIO VISUAL AIDS PLANNED: ___ FLIPCHART(S)   ___ TRANSPARENCY(IES)
                                       ___ 35MM SLIDE(S)   ___ VIDEOTAPE
                                       ___ HANDOUTS   _____ OTHER

FIGURE 6-1:
Introductory Section of the Key Point Summarizer

Figure 6-1 shows the introductory section of the summarizer.

The balance of the summarizer consists of the five essential elements of a successful business presentation: (1) power opener, (2) connector, (3) main body, (4) power close, and (5) anticipating audience questions. To help increase the efficiency of your presentation, this portion of the summarizer is divided into two columns. The left column, "Summary Points," lets you fill in the major points you want to cover in that area. The right column, "Visual Aids," allows space for any audiovisual aids you may wish to include. Figure 6-2 shows a sample of two of these elements: the power opener and the connector. Figure 6-3 shows the section of the summarizer dealing with the main body. Figure 6-4 shows the fourth section of the summarizer, which is for your power close.

The final section of the summarizer (shown in Figure 6-5) helps you highlight in advance possible audience questions, together with an appropriate response for each. While this can never automatically guarantee a perfect question-and-answer session, it does place you, the speaker, in a very effective position and is certainly worth the few moments spent in its preparation.

SUMMARY POINTS	VISUAL AIDS
1. *Power Opener:*	
2. *Connector:*	

FIGURE 6-2:
Sections 1 and 2 of the Summarizer

TITLE OF PRESENTATION: _____

DATE GIVEN: _____

SUMMARY POINTS	VISUAL AIDS
3. *Main Body:*	

FIGURE 6-3:
Section 3 of the Summarizer

TITLE OF PRESENTATION: _____
DATE GIVEN: _____

SUMMARY POINTS	VISUAL AIDS
4. *Power Close:*	

FIGURE 6-4:
Section 4 of the Summarizer

TITLE OF PRESENTATION: _____
DATE GIVEN: _____

	Possible Audience Questions	Appropriate Responses
1.		
2.		

FIGURE 6-5:
Final Section of the Summarizer

Putting the Summarizer into Action: A Sample Presentation

To help you better visualize how to use the summarizer, let's look at a completed filled-in sample. Figure 6-6 shows information for a new product introduction (at the annual sales meeting) of Better Gardens Ltd., a high quality producer of home-gardening equipment. Slides were used by the speaker as an audiovisual aid to the speech, which was expected to last between forty-five minutes and an hour.

The thrust of the talk was to introduce the "Spade-Master" which would be available for sale in all retail outlets in the next month. High hopes had been pinned on this new gardening spade, which, due to its several unique features (including price) should make it one of the leading products of Better Gardens Ltd.

The business presentation was being given by the sales manager to all company distributors and regional sales managers.

Speaker Tips:

- Note that the key point summarizer, when utilized properly, serves as a handy outline for your presentation—it is not intended for you to compile your actual written talk onto the four pages.
- As you become more comfortable with this and the other forms used in this workbook, you may wish to further customize the sample forms for your own specific use.
- Once you have completed the outline of your talk using the summarizer, you will have a concise summary of all the key points you wish to present to your audience—and a clear idea of what audiovisual aids, if any, you will use to get your points across.
- The summarizer has been specifically designed to be inconspicuous. Merely place the pages (unstapled) on the lectern (or even on the table in front of you, if no lectern is available) and after completing each section, merely *slide* each page from left to right. The audience will hardly notice your slight hand movement!
- In certain cases (such as a *very brief* presentation), you may find it easier to make each of your major headings on index cards. Experience has shown however that use of the key point summarizer will be far more efficient) Special Note: in *no circumstance, should you ever use index-cards and the summarizer during the same talk.* It will only serve to confuse you ... since the same info as you would put on index cards is already built into the summarizer.
- If you are the first (or only) speaker, to facilitate the presentation, you

---

KEY POINT SUMMARIZER

TITLE OF PRESENTATION: *Introduction to the "Spade Master" The sales leader for 1988-89!*

DATE GIVEN: *March 2, 1988*

ANTICIPATED DURATION: *Approx. 1 Hour*

FORMAL INTRODUCTION: ___ YES ___ NO   INFORMAL INTRODUCTION: _X_ YES ___ NO

ROOM DIMENSIONS: *85' x 100' (approx.)*   AUDIENCE SIZE: *125 (approx.)*

FAMILIAR WITH AUDIENCE? _X_ YES ___ NO

TYPE OF AUDIO VISUAL AIDS PLANNED: ___ FLIPCHART(S)   ___ TRANSPARENCY(IES)

_X_ 35MM SLIDE(S)   ___ VIDEOTAPE

___ HANDOUTS   _____ OTHER

SUMMARY POINTS	VISUAL AIDS
1. *Power Opener:* *Get ready for the 1988 sales leader!* • *The Spade Master, Model 98* • *Results of 5 years research* • *Will add 25% to distributor profits in first 12 months* • *Definitely a sales leader for years to come!*	SLIDE 1 • *Shot of new model* SLIDE 2 • *Results of consumer research* • *25% additional profit*
2. *Connector:* *MARKET IS READY FOR IT!* • *No other comparable spade can sell for under $12 retail* • *National/local advertising* • *10-year guarantee (first of its kind in the industry)*	SLIDE 3 • *Unbeatable price!* SLIDE 4 • *Heavy advertising support* • *10-year guarantee* • *A great value!*

FIGURE 6-6:
The Key Point Summarizer (Filled-in Sample)

TITLE OF PRESENTATION: *Introduction to the "Spade Master"*
The sales leader for 1988-89!
DATE GIVEN: *March 2, 1988*

SUMMARY POINTS	VISUAL AIDS
3. *Main Body:*	SLIDE 5
	Sizzling Features!
Exciting new features	• *Teflon (no stick)*
• *Teflon coated*	• *Handle is heavily reinforced*
• *Reinforced handle*	• *Unbeatable at $11.99*
• *Retail price of only $11.99 !*	• *Bright aluminum finish*
• *Lightweight (only 4 lbs)*	• *Only 4 lbs*
• *All aluminum construction*	
	SLIDE 6
Great consumer benefits	• *The best tool, at the best price...*
• *Perfect utility tool for every gardener*	*...means top dollar sales for*
• *So light, even a child can use it*	*YOU !!*
• *Practically unbreakable*	
• *Best price/value on the market*	
	SLIDE 7
	Distributor Marketing Push
New distributor marketing policy	• *Co-op ads available*
• *15 % co-op adv. allowance*	• *Better volume discounts*
• *40 % discount on orders of 50 or*	• *In-store displays*
more spades	• *Point of sale bins*
• *Free in-store displays and floor bins*	

FIGURE 6-6:
(continued)

TITLE OF PRESENTATION: *Introduction to the "Spade Master" The sales leader for 1988-89!*

DATE GIVEN: *March 2, 1988*

SUMMARY POINTS	VISUAL AIDS
4. Power Close: *Let's make it happen!* *• Order now for April delivery* *• Extra profits at your doorstep* *• Volume discounts* *• Heavy marketing support*	*SLIDE 8* *Making It Happen* *• Everything going for us!* *Special incentives for volume orders*
Advertising Push *• Ads in BETTER HOMES & GARDENS, GARDENING WORLD, NATIONAL HOME GARDENER plus 15 local magazines and newspapers*	*SLIDE 9* *Fabulous Advertising Support* *• Major newspaper and gardening magazines*
Summary *• Act now for blockbuster spring sales profits* *• First come, first served!* *• Make sure to sign up before leaving meeting!*	*SLIDE 10* *Let's Move !!!* *• Avoid disappointment and lost profits* *• Order now!*

FIGURE 6-6:
(continued)

TITLE OF PRESENTATION: *Introduction to the "Spade Master"*
The sales leader for 1988-89!
DATE GIVEN: *March 2, 1988*

	Possible Audience Questions	Appropriate Responses
1.	*How can you guarantee delivery by next month? After all, you have been late with other promises before!*	*Actually, the new units are ready now... and are only awaiting shipping cartons which are due in next week.*
2.	*I like the new ad campaign. Where can I get the complete list of publications?*	*The schedules are available in the back of the room.*
3.	*I plan to order at least 100 spades. How do I get a better discount?*	*Yes, large quantity discounts are available. Please see your Regional Sales Manager.*
4.	*The 10-year guarantee sounds fantastic. Are you certain that the company will back us up on this?*	*You have our word on it! And we have made good on all promises for the past 25 years!*
5.		

FIGURE 6-6:
(continued)

Speaker Tips (continued):

> should leave your key point summarizer on the lectern *just prior* to the talk. (If you are the second or third speaker, use your judgement!)
> - Always make certain that the summarizer is either typed or filled out in dark ink. (In heavy glare or poor lighting, pencil notes become very difficult to read.)

Six Benefits of Using the Summarizer

1. The summarizer will save valuable time in organizing your talk—from preplanning through final delivery and post-talk evaluation.
2. It offers a clear correlation between what is to be presented and (where applicable) the supporting audiovisual media with which it is used.
3. The summarizer offers a condensed, permanent record of your presentation, which can easily be stored for future reference.
4. When used in conjunction with the Pretalk Room Checklist (Form 00, see Chapter 1), it helps ensure a well-formulated talk.
5. The question-and-answer section will prepare you for the majority of audience questions—and help you anticipate appropriate responses.
6. The summarizer is designed to be as flexible as possible, so you can modify the form wherever required. For example:
   a. Headings could be expanded to list the introducer's name.
   b. When several speakers are conducting the presentation, each name could be listed (with order of presentation and approximate time for each segment).
   c. Each of the headings in the summarizer (Power Opener, Connector, Main Body, Power Close and Audience Questions/Appropriate Responses) can be expanded or constricted, depending on the structure of your presentation. For example, you may want to expand the power opener section to be a full page. Or, you may want to add several pages to the audience questions section.

Chapter Summary

You have now finished a review of the heart of your presentation: the key point summarizer. Starting with a simplified guide on how to complete the form, you reviewed the summarizer in action with a sample business presentation followed by tips for its use and the benefits derived from it.

Now would be an ideal time to proceed directly into the next chapter which illustrates four additional business presentation examples. As you review each one, take special note in how the key point summarizer provides a base of continuity and orderliness, enhanced by its own simplicity of use.

Memory Joggers

☑ The key point summarizer consists of the following sections: (1) The power opener, (2) connectors, (3) main body, (4) close and (5) possible audience questions together with appropriate responses.

☑ The summarizer begins with the required base information that must be considered prior to the development of the talk.

☑ While delivering your presentation, after completing each section of the summarizer, you need only to slide each page from left to right on the lectern. This inconspicuous movement, which the audience will hardly notice, will give your talk a more professional look.

☑ During a presentation, *never* combine the use of index cards with the summarizer. (Experience has shown that employing the keypoint summarizer is far more effective.

☑ Always make certain that the summarizer is completed in dark ink or type. If done in pencil, it may be difficult to read in poor light or glare.

☑ Continue experimenting with customizing the key point summarizer for your specific type of presentation. Remember, the more you adapt the form for your own use, the more effective the presentation is likely to be.

CHAPTER 7

Four Typical Business Presentation Examples

This chapter illustrates how presentations in four typical business categories can be successfully delivered before an audience.

1. An Annual Divisional Review
2. New Bonus Plan Implementation
3. Strategic Business Plan
4. Early Retirement Planning

For maximum benefit, our strategy provides the following format:

- Selection of a suitable classification category (to inform, to motivate, or to persuade)
- What to emphasize
- Pitfalls to avoid
- Background summary data for the talk itself
- Illustration of the talk via the Key Point Summarizer

Whether or not your business presentation is on one of the subjects discussed, you will see how easy it is to adapt the summarizer to virtually any business situation.

Let's begin with a business presentation on a topic that is becoming increasingly more important regardless of company size or industry grouping.

The Annual Divisional Review

Category

Based on the Strategy Classification Chart (see Figure 1-1), this type of talk would be placed under the category of *to inform.*

What to Emphasize

Major emphasis would focus on:

- Keeping the talk highly factual but interesting
- Having the presentation retain a crisp quality through effective pacing and appropriate audiovisual support (where required)
- Using a continuous stream of benefits which applies both to the business and to all employees of the organization.

Secondary emphasis would be to present the material as factually and as neutral as possible. At no time may the audience perceive any type of insincerity or "high pressure" from you, or the validity of your entire presentation may be in jeopardy.

Pitfalls to Avoid

During the presentation, possible cautions could include:

- Avoiding the trap of thinking that everyone in the audience will be in full agreement with what is said. (Keep in mind that silence from the audience does not necessarily mean that the audience approves of your message!)
- Using humor. Due to the serious and important nature of the subject matter, you should deliberately stay away from jokes or any type of lighthearted ad-libbing. Humor can be effective for other types of speeches, but not this one.
- Showing favoritism or taking sides. Remember that, due to the sensitive nature of the topic, people's careers could be affected by what is being proposed in the Divisional Review. Take precautions during your presentation to be as impartial as possible in presenting facts and figures, and to show no favoritism (implied or explicit) to any one group or department.

The Framework

Preplanning: Consider your audience in particular. You want to develop their attention through such positive statements in your power opener as:

- A highly enthusiastic lead-in
- Announcement of recently completed best year in company history
- New highly experienced management place in team
- Now ready for even bigger and better growth opportunities

Attention/Interest: This can be heightened through connectors stressing:

- Plans for greater market penetration
- Heavy national advertising reinforcement
- New product introductions

Main Body: You would probably want to cover specifics on such topics as:

- Stability of the management team
- New growth opportunities
- Anticipated higher sales through new products
- Outpacing of competition
- Reinforcement that you have the best sales force in the industry
- Offering self-motivation to your audience with a clear signal that "all is well"—and will continue to be so.

Desire and Action: Include in your power close such points as:

- You are now in position to become "Number 1" in the industry
- Success rests directly with each member of the sales force
- Within two weeks, each person will receive new sales goals from their regional managers
- You're counting on a 100 percent goal accomplishment from every member of the sales force

Forms and Other Aids to Use

In addition to the Key Point Summarizer, the following forms and figures should help make your task easier in preparing your talk:

- Pretalk Room Checklist
- Strategy Classification Chart
- Presentation Classifications Model

While this system may appear a bit cumbersome to first-time users, rest assured that with just a bit of practice you will learn to proceed rapidly through all the forms in this book with a minimum of effort. Most important, use of this method will make every presentation more effective than the one before!

Also, remember that the data given here and in the other sample presentations are meant only as a guideline.

Background Data for Sample Presentation

The Marnan Company is a national manufacturer and distributor of physical fitness equipment for both home and commercial use (gyms, health salons, etc.). The product is sold mainly through jobbers and authorized distributors.

Figure 7-1 shows how the chairman of the board for the Marnan Company used the key point summarizer to prepare his presentation.

KEY POINT SUMMARIZER

TITLE OF PRESENTATION: *The Marnan Company 1987 Annual Divisional Review*
DATE GIVEN: *January 7, 1988*
ANTICIPATED DURATION: *45 min. to 1 hour*
FORMAL INTRODUCTION: _X_ YES ___ NO   INFORMAL INTRODUCTION: ___ YES ___ NO
ROOM DIMENSIONS: *70' X 90'(Approx.)*   AUDIENCE SIZE: *150 (Approx.)*
FAMILIAR WITH AUDIENCE? _X_ YES ___ NO
TYPE OF AUDIO VISUAL AIDS PLANNED: ___ FLIPCHART(S)   ___ TRANSPARENCY(IES)
_X_ 35MM SLIDE(S)   _X_ VIDEOTAPE
___ HANDOUTS   _____ OTHER

SUMMARY POINTS	VISUAL AIDS
1. Power Opener: *A Great Past/An Even Better Future* • *1987 Best Sales Year to Date* • *New management team in place* • *Emphasis now on stability, not change!* • *Everyone in room will share in growth and new opportunities*	SLIDE 1 • *3-year sales history* • *5-year forecast* SLIDE 2 • *Emphasis on stability* SLIDE 3 • *Profitable partnership*
2. Connector: *Timing is Perfect* • *New market penetration study* • *Heavy advertising support* • *Have identified target markets* • *We have the new products at the right price*	SLIDE 4 *Timing* • *Know target market* • *Advertise heavily* • *New products* • *Competitive pricing*

FIGURE 7-1:
Annual Divisional Review (Filled-in Sample of Summarizer)

TITLE OF PRESENTATION: The Marnan Company 1987 Annual Divisional Review
DATE GIVEN: January 7, 1988

SUMMARY POINTS	VISUAL AIDS
3. *Main Body:*	SLIDE 5 Strategies • Management stability • New product intro • Growth opportunities • Outspace competition
Team Stability • Now in place • No further changes planned • Stronger than ever	
New Products • Best products on market • Right price • No competition • Heavy major advertising • New product demos right after lunch • Growth potential fantastic	SLIDE 6 "Secret Weapon" • We have the best sales and marketing team in the industry
Secret Weapon • We have always been successful and intend to keep it that way. Being the best is tough work — and we are tough!	

FIGURE 7-1:
(continued)

KEY POINT SUMMARIZER (Continued)

TITLE OF PRESENTATION: _The Marnah Company 1987 Divisional Review_
DATE GIVEN: _January 7, 1988_

SUMMARY POINTS	VISUAL AIDS
4. Power Close:	SLIDE 7
	Factors for success
Success	• Motivation
• Within our grasp	• Drive
• Becoming number 1	• Reaching assigned goals
• Team effort	• Teamwork
Make It Happen	SLIDE 8
• Realistic sales goals	Let's go for it
• Opportunities	• Time is now
• Challenges	• Counting on everyone in room
Commitment	SLIDE 9
• Let's do it together	• Number 1 all the way!
• We can count on each other	
Summary	
• We have been the best	CONCLUDE WITH VIDEOTAPE
• We will stay the best	
• We are Number 1	

FIGURE 7-1:
(continued)

TITLE OF PRESENTATION: *The Marnan Company 1987 Divisional Review*
DATE GIVEN: *January 7, 1988*

	Possible Audience Questions	Appropriate Responses
1.	*How do we know that things will finally settle down here?*	*See no reason for any additional changes to occur. You have my word on that— and I intend to keep it!*
2.	*Delighted with the new advertising campaign, but will it be on time this year?*	*Actually, it's already prepared and ready to go at a moment's notice!*
3.	*When will we receive our assigned goals for next year?*	*All regional managers now have goals for their entire region. A date for the goal review will be set up before you leave the hotel.*
4.		
5.		

FIGURE 7-1:
(continued)

The 19X8 annual divisional review presentation is being given by the chairman of the board to the 125-person sales force at the annual offsite meeting on a resort island off the coast of Florida. While sales for the past year have been excellent, the organization has continually suffered from frequent reorganizations of senior management and major operating groups. The result has been a heavier than normal turnover of salesforce, some lowering of morale, and an increasing wave (though highly discreet) of cynicism from salespeople that the company has lost its identity and sense of direction.

Sample Power Openers

"Good morning everyone . . . nice to be with you this morning. As Frank just mentioned in his introduction, we seem to have everything going for us today. A beautiful hotel, nice weather and a day promised to bring you even better things. Well, as your first speaker, I'm ready to begin building further on these nice events. Let's go!"

and

"No one in this room likes to experience change—especially when it happens too often. In the case of our senior management, most of the change resulted from several key members who had reached retirement age, and this was supplemented by another who had decided on early retirement last year, and finally a senior marketing executive who decided to start up his own consulting firm. However, that's all behind us and from this moment on, the emphasis will be on stability and growth . . . You have my promise!"

Sample Connector

"Through careful planning and market timing, the movement towards reaching assigned objectives has never been stronger. Our target market has been identified, the several new products aimed specifically at this market will shortly be introduced, and our pricing and advertising thrust will make us the market leader for years to come!"

Sample Main Body Selections

"I know that you will be as excited as I was when I first viewed our three new outstanding product lines for 1988! Each of these units are priced under $3,000 and contain every feature that, our market research people tell us, the target market really wants! How's that for delivering the right product at the right time to the right people!"

and

"However, most organizations have learned the hard way, that having a saleable product alone isn't a sure-fire guarantee of success. What's also needed is a top-notch sales force . . . something we have known for years! Guess 'the secret' is out . . . we have the best sales team in the industry . . . and intend to keep it that way!"

Sample Power Close

"So . . . our management, production and research teams have done their part to make 1988 a banner year for the Marnan Company. All that remains is to roll out our 'secret weapon' at the conclusion of this conference and watch the sales roll in! I'm counting on every person in this room to do just that! In turn, you have 100 percent of my complete support. A nice combination . . . Don't you think? Thank You."

Sample Questions

Here's a list of typical questions that might be raised at the conclusion of a divisional review.

1. The statistical data presented, and whether it could be skewed to show favorable results
2. The projections given for future sales
3. Analysis of past trends
4. Resurfacing of profitability figures that were presented
5. Questioning of advertising effectiveness and money spent
6. New product development and market research
7. Clarity of next year's marketing objectives
8. Concerns whether the current operating plan is fully in support of the strategic plan
9. Additional discussion on bonuses and incentive pay systems
10. Questions on morale and personnel turnover

Speaker Tips:

Remember that every presenter should:

(1) Consider every question raised as an advantage

(2) Rephrase (or partially rephrase) each question before attempting to answer (this is covered in detail in Chapter 5).

And, in addition, for this particular category of talk;

- Keep the entire presentation crisp, factual and to the point (anything else could be perceived by the audience as indecisive).
- Handouts (if any are used) should be distributed at the *conclusion* of the talk to avoid distractions.
- Since the subject borders on material of a technical nature, heavy use of audiovisual support material is recommended.

Speaker Tips (continued):

> • Make certain in advance, that all anticipated questions have been reviewed and can be answered in a straightforward manner.
> • Maintain eye contact with the audience at all times. Do *not* fall into the trap of "talking to" your flipcharts or screen.
> • Early on in the talk, beware of the trap of talking too fast (as a result of being slightly keyed up). With a bit of discipline, this effect will dissipate rapidly.

To help you in preparing your own presentation, full-page checklists are given at the end of each sample presentation in this chapter. The following checklists offers guidelines in presenting an annual divisional review. (See Chapter 3 for additional help in preparing this type of talk.)

New Bonus Plan Implementation

Our second example of a typical business presentation falls under the heading of *incentive compensation*, a theme that has become increasingly popular among large and small organizations as a reinforcement for positive motivation.

Category
Based on the Strategy Classification Chart, this presentation would fall within both categories of *informing* and *motivating*.

What to Emphasize
Major emphasis should highlight the following:

• Keeping the talk factual but with a heavy infusion of benefits that the new plan will bring
• Building your strategy around being able to secure the audience's attention early and maintaining interest
• Developing your key points to heighten the audience's desire and willingness to accept the new bonus plan as presented

Secondary emphasis would be to develop the presentation in the most impartial way possible while stressing benefits.

Pitfalls to Avoid

• Avoid any inference of "peer pressure" or the implication that "management always knows best."
• Be aware that not everyone will be in complete agreement with all of the elements you present (such as how bonuses are calculated, degree of seniority involved, etc.).

Checklist for Preparing an Annual Divisional Review

Goal Accomplishment
State the major accomplishments vs. assigned goals for the past year

1.

2.

3.

List here (if applicable) those goals that were not reached, and the reasons why

List the planned strategic goals to be reached for the coming year

1.

2.

3.

What obstacles are anticipated, and what strategies will be used to overcome these roadblocks?

Industry Analysis
What was the company's track record this year as compared to the industry average?

The same analysis for the past five years:

How profitable is our company as compared to the competition?

What share of the market can we claim this year?

As against last year?

Projected for the next five years?

Checklist for Preparing an Annual Divisional Review (*Continued*)

Sales/Marketing
What percent of our overall sales are represented by products we introduced during the past 12 months?

What is the projection for next year? Next five years?

As compared to our three leading competitors . . .
— Advertising effectiveness
— Percentage of dollars spend on market research
— Number of people employed in the direct sales force
— Number of wholesalers/distributors
— Number of retail outlets selling the product
— Total number of people employed in the marketing capacity

What is our secondary strategy if we are not on target at the end of the first quarter?

Economics
What is the price elasticity for our products?

Should we continue to manufacture in this country, or look to less expensive labor markets abroad?

What are the trade-off's involved?

What is the economic forecast for the next 12 months, and how will that affect us?

Staffing
Staff headcount (this year vs. last year)

Total number of exempt employees

Total number of non-exempt staff

List any changes (if any) in the current salary and incentive programs

Review here (if applicable) any outstanding compliance issues

- Pace your presentation carefully to help keep the mood positive. Although your intent is to create a groundswell of positive motivation, you might have just the reverse take place.

The Framework

Preplanning: Since you plan to both inform and motivate, it makes good sense to keep the talk factual, but (at the same time), highly *upbeat*. Keep in mind that the heavy use of *positive* body language is *crucial* throughout the presentation (such as a relaxed posture and a warm genuine smile) versus an inadvertent frown or hands jammed in pockets). Key points to remember include:

- An early WIFM in the talk will definitely enhance this type of presentation.
- Use audiovisual as much as possible (to heighten interest) and avoid any misunderstanding of numbers or concepts.
- Be prepared for many questions at conclusion of talk.
- Remember (especially in this type of presentation), audience silence does not necessarily mean consent.

Attention: Capture your audience's attention early through creative use of the power opener. For example:

- An enthusiastic yet clearly responsive message delivered by the national sales manager.
- A brief history of the organization's compensation system and the clear need for change.
- The fact that, when required, senior management can react swiftly to field problems . . . and in the next thirty minutes it will be proven to them!

Interest: Use connectors stressing such ideas as:

- Plans for increased company growth next year
- Key to field sales success rests with each zone manager
- The next thirty minutes will prove the organization's commitment to its sales force.

Highlight plan specifics in the main body with the following:

- Overall incentive plan concept
- How bonus was tied to percentage increase over a previous three-year average
- Examples of special situations where adjustments might be necessary (such as a new sales territory being created)
- Specific examples (via actual numbers) on the payout features of the plan
- Plan was designed by the three regional sales directors

Desire and action: Reinforce these through the power close using the following points.

- At close of meeting, each regional director would meet with all zone managers to supply additional examples of how the new system would work, and answer any questions.
- Senior management backs the new plan 100 percent and has given the national sales manager complete autonomy in running it.
- Within the next two days, each of the zone managers will have an opportunity to review the projected three-year base average with his or her regional director and to discuss (and resolve) any special situations that might arise during discussion of the numbers.
- A fairer compensation system was requested, and senior management came through for the "troops." Now the stage is set for one of the best sales years to date. The company is counting on each sales manager to do exactly that!

Background Data for Sample Presentation

XYZ Company represents a complete line of home-improvement services covering three northeastern states. While the national headquarters is located in Pennsylvania, the firm maintains both distribution and sales offices in key cities there and in several locations within New York and New Jersey.

All three states are considered as independent regions, with each having sales representatives (covering a specified territory) reporting to zone managers. In turn, these managers report to the regional sales director for the state. These three directors report directly to the national sales manager.

There has never been a compensation problem with the local sales representatives. Each of them is paid on a straight salary plus commission basis, with all field expenses reimbursed at 100 percent. The inequity that has arisen (hence, the need for the bonus plan) has been with the 18 zone managers, who traditionally have been paid on straight salary with no type of override or incentive compensation. As a result, while the company has grown significantly in sales volume, there have been important differences in the amount achieved among certain territories. During the past several months, many zone managers have expressed dissatisfaction with the system, claiming the need for some type of bonus plan based on performance. From every aspect, their claim was justified. An incentive bonus plan was developed as follows:

1. Each zone manager was to receive a quota based on the last three-year sales average.
2. This new quota would be for a twelve-month period, with a six-month "payout" feature (in effect, a "draw" against the anticipated bonus).
3. The incentive compensation structure would be simple, fair, and easy to calculate.
4. Bonus arrangements on all increases over five percent would be at the discretion of the national sales manager.

5. While this would be based on a smaller dollar payout (bonus to percentage of increase), it had the potential to increase significantly a zone manager's total compensation package.

6. The new bonus plan contained the implication that each zone manager was expected to increase sales for the assigned territories—and to be reimbursed accordingly. If no increase was forthcoming, a zone manager's career could be in jeopardy.

The presentation was delivered by the national sales manager, who aimed to inform while stressing the motivational aspects of the new bonus plan and senior management's quick response to the field request for some type of incentive compensation program. Further, a clear vote of confidence was needed from the 18 zone managers. The three regional directors helped to create the main elements of the plan and were in full support of it.

For preplanning purposes, the presentation would occur on the second day of a four-day marketing conference. This was traditionally held semi-annually at the organization's executive office in Philadelphia.

Speaker Tips:

Presenting a New Plan

- Due to the somewhat technical nature of the subject (involving bonuses, performance figures, etc.), heavy use of audiovisual aids is recommended. Handouts will reinforce your points and serve as a valuable reference tool later on.

- Get to the point right way. In the power opener you should clearly state the point of your talk, and let the audience know that you are in favor of the new plan.

- Due to the sensitive nature of the topics, avoid a formal introduction. Instead, employ (if possible) a relatively informal one.

- Walk the rather fine line between being very factual but "not stiff" ... neutral as possible without appearing biased in any manner.

- Try to have all questions held until the end of the talk; otherwise, you may be frequently interrupted with the presentation in danger of losing continuity.

- Maintain continuous eye contact with the audience; in no way do you want to appear as being aloof.

- Where appropriate, use the technique of pausing right before making key points ... this will heighten audience interest.

KEY POINT SUMMARIZER

TITLE OF PRESENTATION: *Revised Sales Force Compensation Plan*
DATE GIVEN: *May 10, 1988*
ANTICIPATED DURATION: *1 hour (approx.)*
FORMAL INTRODUCTION: ___ YES ___ NO   INFORMAL INTRODUCTION: X YES ___ NO
ROOM DIMENSIONS: *70' x 100' (approx.)*   AUDIENCE SIZE: *43 (approx.)*
FAMILIAR WITH AUDIENCE? X YES ___ NO
TYPE OF AUDIO VISUAL AIDS PLANNED: ___ FLIPCHART(S)   X TRANSPARENCY(IES)
                                        X 35MM SLIDE(S)   ___ VIDEOTAPE
                                        ___ HANDOUTS   _____ OTHER

SUMMARY POINTS	VISUAL AIDS
1. Power Opener: COMPENSATION SURVEY COMPLETED — FINALLY HAVE EQUITABLE SYSTEM • Need for compensating sales force based on performance • Old system unfair, held together by "band-aids and glue" • Four-month compensation study by outside consultants now complete • Entire sales force will benefit	SLIDE 1 • Inadequate field compensation/system SLIDE 2 • Shot of band-aids on old tire (with many patches) SLIDE 3 • Short bio of consulting firm
2. Connector: SYSTEM AVAILABLE FOR IMPLEMENTATION NEXT MONTH • Will begin in four weeks • Heavy emphasis given to new account openings and net sales increase by territory • All sales representatives will now be compensated solely on merit • All "house accounts" now being turned back to sales reps	SLIDE 4 • Start date in four weeks • New account openings and net sales increases highlighted SLIDE 5 • Compensation system based strictly on performance • All current house accounts reverting back to territory

FIGURE 7-2:
Sales Force Compensation Plan (Filled-in Sample of Summarizer)

TITLE OF PRESENTATION: _Revised Sales Force Compensation Plan_
DATE GIVEN: _May 10, 1988_

SUMMARY POINTS	VISUAL AIDS

3. Main Body:
 	
PLAN HIGHLIGHTS
• Net sales average for each territory based on last 3-year average
• "Special situations" i.e., dealer going bankrupt, sudden windfalls, etc., will be judged on individual basis
• Each sales rep to receive base salary and incentive compensation per following schedule
  – Base salary upon achieving sales average for past three years
  – For each 10% of additional net sales achieved, 5% additional over base salary paid out
  – By obtaining a 100% increase in sales, a rep would achieve a substantial increase in total compensation
  – Payouts made every 6 months (with a 15% reserve withheld)
	TRANSPARENCY 1
	• 3-year average for base computation
	• Special situations to be reviewed
	
	TRANSPARENCY 2
	Schedule
	• Base = 3-year average
	• Each 10% of all sales = 5% additional compensation over base
	
	TRANSPARENCY 3 (Example)
	• Base = salary $40,000
	• Sales average $1,000,000
	• Net sales increase of 20% = $200,000 (or $1,200,000)
	• Extra compensation = $10,000
	• Net compensation:
	  Base salary $40,000
	  Extra comp. <u>10,000</u>
	  Total comp. 50,000

FIGURE 7-2:
(continued)

TITLE OF PRESENTATION: <u>Revised Sales Force Compensation Plan</u>
DATE GIVEN: <u>May 10, 1988</u>

SUMMARY POINTS	VISUAL AIDS
4. Power Close:	*SLIDE 6*
	• More equitable
<u>BENEFITS OF NEW PLAN</u>	• Merit is the key
• Much fairer than before	• Incentive system works best
• Pay based heavily on merit	
• Incentive system has always proven more effective with sales people	*SLIDE 7*
	• Plan jointly worked out by senior sales management and executive committee
<u>MANAGEMENT APPROVAL</u>	• Now ready to roll!
• Review by executive committee and all key sales VPs	• All systems go!
• Plan ready for implementation within 4 weeks	*SLIDE 8*
• Data processing ready to enter system on computer within next 10 days	• Next 4 weeks critical
	• Goal and instruction forms available during next 15 days
	• "Hot line" open for next 6 weeks on confidential basis
<u>COMMUNICATION TO FIELD SALES FORCE</u>	
• Should be done by all regional sales managers within next 4 weeks	*SLIDE 9*
• Home office "hot line" will open for 6 weeks to handle any questions on confidential basis	• You wanted it . . .
• New goal forms available in 2 weeks for distribution to all sales managers	• We did it . . .
	• Now, let's go!
<u>SUMMARY</u>	
• You asked for a better pay system—now you have it. Let's go out there and really show what a great sales team we have!	

FIGURE 7-2:
(continued)

KEY POINT SUMMARIZER (Continued)

TITLE OF PRESENTATION: _Revised Sales Force Compensation Plan_

DATE GIVEN: _May 10, 1988_

	Possible Audience Questions	Appropriate Responses
1.	Did these outside consultants receive any special instructions or limitations from our management group? If so, what were they?	There were none at all. The consultants had a free hand in appraising our current compensation system and in making unbiased, appropriate recommendations.
2.	Regarding management approval, who represented the opinion of the sales force? After all, they are crucial to the process.	I completely agree. The committee consisted of the vice-president of marketing, the vice-president of sales and five of the ten regional sales managers.
3.	What happens if there is a disagreement between the sales rep and his/her manager over the 3-year base average?	If this occurs, the situation will be arbitrated by the vice-president of sales.
4.	Are you certain that the new goal forms will be available in the next two weeks?	Yes. In fact, they should be ready by next week at the latest
5.	How can you guarantee that all calls to the "hot line" will be confidential?	Very simple. The consulting firm who designed our system will lend us part-time staff to answer these calls. Frankly, they could care less who the people are that call!

FIGURE 7-2:
(continued)

Sample Power Openers

"Good Morning! Since we all know each other, I didn't feel that a formal introduction was necessary. And, since time means money to all of us, let's get right to the point. Listen very carefully, for in the next thirty minutes, I will show you a new compensation plan that is fair, motivational, and designed especially for you."

and

"Thanks for coming this morning. Since I am personally familiar with everyone in this room, you know from experience that I always come right to the point. Let's put it this way. We had an unfair compensation plan for zone managers. You spoke up. Now we fixed it. In my opinion, this plan is terrific."

Sample Connector

"In the next thirty minutes or so, you will hear the details of a new incentive compensation plan that is ready to be put into use immediately, has the full support of senior management, and should certainly add to your income this year—as the company continues to expand. Fair enough?"

Sample Main Body Selections

"Now, in the first place, the plan was designed by your regional managers . . . people who have come up through the ranks just as I did. Sure enough, when we took a close look at the past five years' sales versus income, you were correct. Some glaring inequities did exist, and this provided us with an excellent rationale on where to make the adjustments. In other words, just another example of how when you talk, we listen!"

and

"We intend to be quite flexible in administering the plan. We recognize the fact that adjustments will be necessary from time to time. At the same time, we do expect a superior sales effort from each of you. Put another way, let's go out and make more sales, and also put more money in our pockets. Sound OK to you?"

Sample Power Close

"Well, that's more than enough talk from me. Now it's your turn. Each of the regions has been assigned a 'breakout room' to review the details of the plan in greater depth. During the next two days, you will each have a chance to review your quota in detail.

"Now, let's get started. Are you ready? Let's go!"

Sample Questions

Here are some typical questions that could be raised at the conclusion of a revised sales force compensation plan:

1. Why are we changing the current system?
2. Specifically, how is the proposed system better than our current plan?

Checklist for Presenting a New Bonus Plan

Briefly state the history of your organization's system. Why does it need to change?

Who created the new plan? Why? State briefly a summary of what the new plan offers. (Highlights)

List three examples where adjustments may be necessary after the new bonus plan is implemented.

1.

2.

3.

What kind of monetary benefit will result from the new bonus plan?

What drawbacks, if any, might employees be concerned with?

How many people are eligible to receive this particular type of bonus?

Is seniority a factor in determining bonuses? Why or why not?

How are the bonuses calculated?

Is the bonus system simple to understand?

When will the plan be in effect?

List three examples where this plan is specifically better than the current one

1.

2.

3.

What is the procedure if a disagreement occurs? Who has the final sign-off in the system?

3. Will the proposed new system cost us more money? If so, how much?

4. How does this new system compare to our main competitors?

5. How long will it take to implement this system?

6. Who designed this system? Were they qualified?

7. Have you projected our costs for the proposed system over the next five years? Ten years?

8. How simple would it be to make adjustments to the system, once implemented?

9. Does the proposed plan conflict in any way with the new tax laws?

10. Who will monitor this new system to insure fairness?

Strategic Business Plan

This third example of a business presentation takes us to the rather specialized but quite common area of presenting a formal strategic business plan to both peers and superiors. Unlike our previous example of the new bonus plan, a talk of this type is usually more difficult to present. As shown on the strategy classification chart this type of talk would be under the category of *to inform*.

What to Emphasize

To be successful, the major focus of this talk would be to:

1. *Inform* the audience of the pertinent facts and figures regarding the proposed business strategy.

2. *Motivate* the divisional executives (or whomever has final approval regarding acceptance of the plan) that the proposals put forth in the presentation are based on sound business judgments and are the correct course of action to follow.

3. *Persuade* the decision makers to approve the plan as presented, with a minimum of prolonged discussion, extensive questions being raised, and other distracting (but sometimes necessary) roadblocks to overcome before final approval is given.

Pitfalls to Avoid

- If more than one person will be presenting, each should clearly define his or her role to the audience prior to the actual talk. All speakers should practice beforehand to ensure a smooth "pass off" from one speaker to the next.

- Make certain that everyone in the audience has a clear view of the speaker, the screen or other props that might be used—or you will find the audience "tuning you out" while you are presenting.

- Keep your presentation lively, informative, yet open-ended enough to allow for a lively question-and-answer session at the end of the talk. Your audience must not perceive that the presentation is one-sided.

The Framework

Preplanning: All preplanning focuses on the goal of *high professionalism* in delivering the talk. Accordingly, special emphasis should be given to:

- Determining what type of introduction will be given so as to develop an effective bridging WIFM/power opener
- The number of presenters (if more than one); clarify the order of speaking and roles played by each speaker
- Heavy use of audiovisual to enhance clarity of presentation and heighten interest in material being presented
- Avoid use of humor (it usually has no place in this type of talk)
- Make certain to "dress for the occasion" (if majority of audience will be in dark blue or black conservative clothing, so should you.
- If possible, trying to hold all questions to the end (frequent questions during the talk can be very distracting to the audience)
- Trying for appropriate body-language (avoid the "stiff-look"); use hand and arm gestures with accompanying varying voice modulation when you want to make a point
- Not assuming that silence in the room insures the fact that most people agree (or understand) with the points you are making. Keep checking for receptiveness and understanding

Attention: Secure the attention of your audience early with an attention-grabbing display such as the following:

- Have the room darkened initially and display the impressive three-year sales history for a few seconds without any comment. Then display a second slide stating: "The first three years were OK— but now watch us grow even more!"
- Immediately turn on the lights and announce the confidence and enthusiasm that the Sales and Marketing team has for the next thirty-six months— and beyond!
- Convey the fact that in the next sixty minutes a marketing plan will be outlined which will show clear direction and strategic initiatives that should be seized for maximum advantage.
- Reinforce the fact that all key members of the Sales and Marketing team participated in the plan and are in complete agreement with it.

Interest: This can be heightened through the connector by emphasizing:

- Where you have been
- Where you are now
- Where you want to be in three years
- How you plan to get there

In the main body focus on such specifics as:

- Overall executive summary of current financial profile
- Senior management key action items
- Short- and long-term opportunities/obstacles
- Future trends in franchising and how to capitalize on them
- Current position—strengths/resources/weaknesses
- Competitive analysis
- Specific recommendations to reach assigned target goals

Desire and action: These are supported through the power close, utilizing the following points:

- The company is now ready to assume expanded market growth in additional four states (for a total of eight).
- Advertising expenditures are being increased by 40 percent, will be completely justified, and are required to support the goal of 30 percent annual growth.
- All expenses to be incurred over the next three years will be mandatory to supply additional staff and facilities required to maintain targeted growth.
- To provide a measurement tool for senior management, formal quarterly reviews will be initiated to measure progress versus goals (which in turn will supplement the current monthly reporting system).
- The Marketing and Sales team are ready to go! All that is needed now is an OK from senior management . . . and the progress will begin.

Forms and other aids to use: The following forms are suggested to help prepare your presentation.

- Strategy Classification Chart
- Pre-Talk Room Checklist
- Presentation Classification Model
- Key Point Summarizer

Background Data for Sample Presentation

The organization is a regional franchiser of a complete line of homemade gourmet ice cream and tofutti stores. Established three years ago by two brothers, the number of stores under franchise has grown from the original three (operated as a family enterprise by the two brothers) to fifty-six stores located in four Midwest states. Revenue is obtained from sales of franchise (fee plus related administrative/ management fees) plus profit derived from both supplying all ingredients/supplies for each location, plus a small percentage royalty on gross sales.

Headquartered in Chicago, the firm has expanded its management team to include several key sales and marketing executives, as well as product specialists who oversee all new product development and quality control. The older brother, Mark Simpson, has become Chairman of the Board, while his younger brother, Charles, assumed the title of President one year ago.

The presentation, covering the three-year strategic business plan (from 1988 to 1990) was given by John Savarese, Vice President of Marketing. Due to the firm's short history and highly rapid growth, this was the first time a strategic business plan was presented in a formal manner. It was a key meeting in every sense of the word, as senior management has already indicated its desire for a minimum annual growth of 30 percent during the next five years.

Sample Power Openers

"Thanks for the impressive introduction, Charles! You really know how to motivate a fellow to give a major talk! As you often said, we should never operate in the dark. But . . . I'm now going to start the presentation by breaking that rule! (Room is darkened, with Slide #1 illuminated). *Now, let's begin by viewing one of the most impressive sales records in the industry!"*

and

"Thanks Charles . . . appreciate the kind words. Since we are all pressed for time, I'll keep the presentation within the allocated sixty minutes . . . but am prepared to stay as long as necessary to handle your questions at the end of the session."

Sample Connector

"We've learned from experience that the most effective way to evaluate a business plan is to consider the four elements that help form the strategy core of any business. This involves a hard look at:

- *Where we have been (our past history)*
- *Where we are now (current status)*
- *Where do we want to go? (goal and objectives)*
- *How do we get there? (operating plan)*

"Sounds rather easy, doesn't it? However, let me assure you that being able to answer all four questions accurately puts one into a category of pure genius! But . . . let's see how good you think we did, after you hear all of the strategies we devised in the plan!"

KEY POINT SUMMARIZER

TITLE OF PRESENTATION: *Gourmets Delight, Ltd. 1988-1990 Strategic Business Plan*
DATE GIVEN: *January 7, 1988*
ANTICIPATED DURATION: *60 minutes (excluding Question and Answer Period)*
FORMAL INTRODUCTION: ___ YES _X_ NO   INFORMAL INTRODUCTION: _X_ YES ___ NO
ROOM DIMENSIONS: *Exec Conf. Room*   AUDIENCE SIZE: *12 to 14 people*
FAMILIAR WITH AUDIENCE? _X_ YES ___ NO
TYPE OF AUDIO VISUAL AIDS PLANNED: ___ FLIPCHART(S)   ___ TRANSPARENCY(IES)
_X_ 35MM SLIDE(S)   ___ VIDEOTAPE
_X_ HANDOUTS   _____ OTHER

SUMMARY POINTS	VISUAL AIDS
1. Power Opener: WE'RE GOOD AND WILL GET BETTER • High confidence level of staff • Marketing plan will show clear direction for continued growth • Creation of plans was a cooperative effort • Next 60 minutes will set direction for next 3 months!	SLIDE 1 (Dark Room) • Sales record for first three years • Display via dramatic upward bar graph SLIDE 2 (Lights on) • Now... "Watch us grow even more!"
2. Connector: THE FOUR QUESTIONS WE NOW FACE • Where we have been • Where we are now • Where do we want to be in 3 years • How we plan to get there	NOTE: Slides 3-6 would each contain main heading and supporting bulleted points for each of the four questions. SLIDE 3 • Past history SLIDE 4 • Current status SLIDE 5 • Three-year objectives SLIDE 6 • Strategy required

FIGURE 7-3:
Strategic Business Plan (Filled-in Sample of Summarizer)

KEY POINT SUMMARIZER (Continued)

TITLE OF PRESENTATION: *Gourmets Delight, Ltd. 1988-1990 Strategic Business Plan*
DATE GIVEN: *January 7, 1988*

SUMMARY POINTS	VISUAL AIDS
3. Main Body:	SLIDE 7 Summary • Gross and net profit picture • Return on equity • Projections for next three years
EXECUTIVE SUMMARY • Current financial profile • Profit margins and projections	
	SLIDE 8 Action Required • Six items needing approval • Staff required
KEY ACTION ITEMS • Approval of budget request • Hiring of 5% additional staff	
	SLIDE 9 Opportunities/Potential Problems • Still unique in field • Expansion still feasible • Competition will become much heavier
OPPORTUNITIES/OBSTACLES • Franchise still unique in industry • Can expand to at least 5 additional states • Profit margin remains high • Competition should be heavy in next 2 years	
	SLIDE 10 Financing Trends • Longer payout required for franchise • Need more creative ways to sell franchise.
TRENDS IN FINANCING • Longer fee payout required • Partnership between company and franchise • More creative finance wanted	
	SLIDE 11 Current Status • Still ahead in consumer taste polls • Must watch cash position • Three-year economic forecast very favorable for industry
CURRENT POSITION • Must not overextend credit lines • Latest survey shows heavy consumer support for product	

FIGURE 7-3:
(continued)

KEY POINT SUMMARIZER (Continued)

TITLE OF PRESENTATION: _Gourmets Delight, Ltd. 1988-1990 Strategic Business Plan_
DATE GIVEN: _January 7, 1988_

SUMMARY POINTS	VISUAL AIDS
3. Main Body:	SLIDE 12 Competition • Only two, but more on horizon
COMPETITIVE ANALYSIS • Ice-Cream Haven • Tofutti King	SLIDE 13 Recommendations • Budget approval • Recruitment of personnel • Advertising increase
RECOMMENDATIONS • Approve budget by January 10th • Begin recruiting within 2 weeks • Start advertising campaign ASAP	

FIGURE 7-3:
(continued)

KEY POINT SUMMARIZER (Continued)

TITLE OF PRESENTATION: *Gourmets Delight, Ltd 1988-1990 Strategic Business Plan*
DATE GIVEN: *January 7, 1988*

SUMMARY POINTS	VISUAL AIDS
4. Power Close:	SLIDE 14
	Expansion overview
READY FOR EXPANSION NOW	• 4 States now
• 4 States targeted	• 30% growth annually
• Advance expenditures +40%	• Need resource backup
• Growth of 30% annually feasible	
	SLIDE 15
STEPS REQUIRED	Action Steps Required
• Budget approval	• Approval of plan
• Set up special 3-day marketing	• Advertising strategy should be
conference to build strategy	implemented ASAP
• Build advertising coverage within	• Offsite conference
next three weeks, expand on new	
strategy	SLIDE 16
	Commitment
MANAGEMENT COMMITMENT	• Vote of confidence will start ball
• Need vote of confidence from senior	rolling
management today	
• Ready to start ball rolling this	
afternoon	

FIGURE 7-3:
(continued)

KEY POINT SUMMARIZER (Continued)

TITLE OF PRESENTATION: _Gourmet's Delight, Ltd. 1988-1990 Strategic Business Plan_
DATE GIVEN: _January 7, 1988_

	Possible Audience Questions	Appropriate Responses
1.	Why the expansion to only 4 states? Why not at least double that figure?	We would be overlooking our resources dangerously—both financially and in people/supply resources required.
2.	Are we certain that latest favorable consumer survey is accurate? Are we okay on this?	Absolutely. HABRO Company considered most reliable in the field. Results are always double-checked.
3.	Why is 5% additional staff needed? Isn't it better to keep staff as small as possible?	Additional staff needed in sales area to market our franchise/ achieving target growth.
4.	Getting a bit worried about competition. Are you sure there are only two major ones?	Difficult to answer specifically. Most likely, there will be 3 to 4 more within next 12 months.
5.	Are you absolutely certain we should move ahead with this plan now?	Yes—quite sure! I wouldn't have proposed it so strongly, if I had any self doubts.

FIGURE 7-3:
(continued)

Sample Main Body Selections

"Note that we have requested an increase of five people representing an approximate annual expense of $400,000. A high expense figure by any standard—but remember that these people will be based in our Sales Department and actually closing deals with franchisees. They will earn every cent given to them—for without their effort, we will not achieve our stated goal increase.

"I've requested our vice president of finance to consider some alternative financing routes for those who want to secure our franchise. The minimum up-front fee of $200,000 is a real obstacle for many of our prospects—who can afford the franchise, but have difficulty with the size of the required deposit. Solving this one problem alone can increase our sales by at least five to ten percent a year!"

Sample Power Close

"It's exactly one hour since I started this presentation, and I'm pleased to say we remained on schedule all the way. All we need now is the official nod from senior management, and we can put the plan in operation immediately. It represents our best thinking, and stands a good chance of achieving every assigned objective set by our management team."

and

"However, I did request that you hold all questions until the conclusion of the talk—and it's obvious that many of you are ready with them now! Let's start by taking one from Frank, who had his hand up first . . ."

Speaker Tips:

Giving a Strategic Business Plan Presentation

- Keep your presentation factual, crisp, and highly professional.
- While you attempt to motivate your audience, be sure not to give any hint of emotionalism or theatrics.
- Schedule the talk strictly within the time allotted by senior management and stick to it. But, do not limit the time for the question and answer session.
- Use audiovisual support to help clarify, expand, and make the heavy use of number reading easier to comprehend. Slides are especially effective.
- Be familiar with the room's setup: check for location of lights, how to handle projector, and other related speaking supports. Don't be caught off guard.

Sample Questions

Here are some representative questions that might be raised at the conclusion of a strategic business plan:

1. Why show our sales growth for only *X* years? Why not for a longer period?
2. And (conversely) why project sales expense for only *X* years? Why not for a longer period?
3. The gross and net profit figures appear distorted. Who can verify them?
4. That is our ranking in the industry? And how are we positioned against our main competitors?
5. What is our market research budget as a percent of sales?
6. Who actually signs off on the strategic business plan?
7. What is the amount we spend on advertising, as compared to our closest competitor?
8. How does our gross margin percentage rank with other similar firms . . . and how can we improve it?
9. Describe the role of human resources in accomplishing the objectives set forth in the plan.
10. When was the last time a consumer research study was done?

(Human Resources Presentation) Early Retirement Planning

Category

Based on the strategy classification chart, this type of talk would fall under all three categories: to inform, motivate and persuade.

What to Emphasize

Major thrust of talk would highlight:

- Keeping the talk interesting, but highly factual.
- Creating the want in the audience (of instituting an early retirement planning system) without being perceived as high pressure.
- Applying heavy use of benefit statements and WIFM throughout talk.
- Keeping in mind the possible audience sensitivity to the subject, and therefore continuing to focus on *need* for the system.

Pitfalls to Avoid

During the talk, some possible cautions might include the following:

- Avoid a patronizing or paternal attitude at all times. Remember, the subject matter is extremely sensitive.

- Stay away from any hint of "high-pressure" on the part of the organization to accomplish this type of planning.
- Never fall into the trap of appearing impatient during the question and answer session. Remember that some people in the audience will have to shortly make a major decision based on the proposal that they will be given.
- Avoid comparing younger employees to their more senior counterparts throughout the entire talk.
- *If possible*, try to use a mature individual as a presenter!

Speaker Tips:

- Don't create an air of false "shock-value"
- Many people might resist the idea ... at first
- Some people may never completely accept the concept
- Subject borders upon age ... always a sensitive issue
- Avoid the pitfall of assumption (never assume everyone is interested in early retirement planning because the organization is sponsoring it). The reverse may also hold true, (where people become suspicious of company motives in sponsoring the plan in the first place.

The Framework

Preplanning:

- Creation of a strong power opener is essential to develop early rapport with audience and gain favorable attention.
- Keep talk impartial and factual; but liberally introduce specific WIFMs.
- Heavy use of audiovisual is recommended, with *benefits* of early retirement planning also shown in a complimentary color.
- Make certain to be continually aware of audience body language during presentation. Note especially where people seem to be concerned or puzzled. Make sure that you go back to these points, if necessary.
- Frequently use benefit statements throughout the entire talk.
- If audience is small (under 15 people), you may want to consider answering questions as they are asked, instead of holding them off to the end.
- Be highly empathetic to the question of age and people's preconceived attitudes towards retirement (it remains a highly sensitive subject).
- Be prepared to be very patient during the question and answer period. Try to anticipate as many audience questions (and their appropriate responses) *beforehand*.

Audience attention would be created through careful use of the power opener, and include

- A strong lead-in by speaker
- Discrete use of shock value (need for system)
- Carefully timed, use of supporting flipchart

Interest would be strengthened through use of the connector, such as:

- Instituting of educational in-house seminars to keep people informed
- Reliance on training department for required logistics
- Need for top management to supply budget and 100 percent support

Desire and action to be boosted by the power close using the following points:

- Steps required right now
- Benefits of moving quickly
- Importance of subject

Forms and other aids to use: To facilitate preparation, this type of talk would rely on the following forms:

- Key Point Summarizer
- Pre-Talk Room Checklist
- Strategy Classification Chart
- Presentation Classification Model

Background Data for Sample Presentation

Muffin Enterprises is a manufacturer of children's toys for children up to 12 years of age. The products are sold mainly through authorized dealers, with certain large retail accounts being handled on a direct basis.

The focus on early retirement planning is being presented by the vice president of Human Resources, and is being given a special time slot at the semi-monthly meeting of the 25 key managers of the firm.

Sales and profits have always been excellent (since the company's founding, 12 years ago), but a small drop in sales is just beginning to occur, due to the heavy competition from foreign imports.

As with many other similar organizations, very little early retirement planning has been put in place, and the need for some should be quite obvious to all.

But is it? And what about the additional expense it will incur . . . in case of a possible long term decline in sales?

Truly, a challenging presentation for the vice president, Human Resources to undertake!

KEY POINT SUMMARIZER

TITLE OF PRESENTATION: _Early Retirement Planning_
DATE GIVEN: _December 18, 1987_
ANTICIPATED DURATION: _15-20 minutes_
FORMAL INTRODUCTION: ___ YES _X_ NO   INFORMAL INTRODUCTION: _X_ YES ___ NO
ROOM DIMENSIONS: _MAIN CONF. ROOM 40'X75'_   AUDIENCE SIZE: _____
FAMILIAR WITH AUDIENCE? _X_ YES ___ NO
TYPE OF AUDIO VISUAL AIDS PLANNED: _X_ FLIPCHART(S)   ___ TRANSPARENCY(IES)
    ___ 35MM SLIDE(S)   ___ VIDEOTAPE
    ___ HANDOUTS   _____ OTHER

SUMMARY POINTS	VISUAL AIDS
1. Power Opener: NEED FOR EARLY RETIREMENT PLAN • Approximately 307, total work force between 40-53 years old (average service, 15 to 20 years) • We have no type of early retirement education program • Many misconceptions arising • Have best work force, but are very poor in communicating	FLIP CHART 1 • Work force statistics • Age and length of service FLIP CHART 2 • No type of education program for early retirement FLIP CHART 3 • Best work force but poorly communicated with
2. Connector: WE MUST NOW ACT QUICKLY • Requires heavy involvement from all line managers • Existing training priorities must be shifted	FLIP CHART 4 • Current challenges that we face

FIGURE 7-4:
Early Retirement Plan (Filled-in Sample of Summarizer)

KEY POINT SUMMARIZER (*Continued*)

TITLE OF PRESENTATION: *Early Retirement Planning*
DATE GIVEN: *December 18, 1987*

SUMMARY POINTS	VISUAL AIDS
3. Main Body:	FLIP CHART 5
	• weekly seminar logistics
INSTITUTING WEEKLY SEMINARS	
• Everyone, 55 and over invited	
• Done as luncheon information sessions	FLIP CHART 6
• Key personnel efforts to speak	• Training department Support
• Sessions kept low-key / informal	(a) personnel
	(b) line management
TRAINING DEPARTMENT INVOLVEMENT	
• Will coordinate luncheon seminars	
• Under direction of personnel manager, will create retirement fact handbooks, flyers, etc.	FLIP CHART 7
	• Required project support
• Design of audiovisual support matierol as requested	
SENIOR MANAGEMENT SUPPORT	
• Management committee in full agreement	
• Have already allocated budget for seminar	
• Will supply periodic guest speakers on tops of mutual interest	

FIGURE 7-4:
(continued)

TITLE OF PRESENTATION: _Early Retirement Planning_
DATE GIVEN: _December 18, 1987_

SUMMARY POINTS	VISUAL AIDS
4. *Power Close:* WHAT'S REQUIRED RIGHT NOW • Select steering committee to guide project through all phases • Identify specific training support required for launch • Letter from president to all employees, announcing program • Coordinate project budget • Identify project manager from personnel department (to coordinate with steering committee) SUMMARY • Program benefits • Commitment to program • Need for fast action	FLIP CHART 8 • Action steps now required FLIP CHART 9 • Summary points

FIGURE 7-4:
(continued)

KEY POINT SUMMARIZER (Continued)

TITLE OF PRESENTATION: _Early Retirement Planning_

DATE GIVEN: _December 18, 1987_

	Possible Audience Questions	Appropriate Responses
1.	Understand need—but why the sudden urgency?	Executive committee has assigned this as top priority. It's a long overdue project and has been badly neglected.
2.	Will any of the required funding be taken out of departmental budgets?	No. All required funding will be drawn from general management fund.
3.	When will all written guidelines on early retirement be available?	Within two weeks from today—at the latest.
4.	Training department currently designing a major program for my department. Does that now mean a delay?	Not necessarily. Training manager will meet with you shortly to review project milestones. Training department has the OK to hire outside consultants on temp. basis.
5.		

FIGURE 7-4:
(continued)

Sample Power Opener

"Good morning, everyone, I appreciate the time given to me to introduce a recommendation on implementing an early retirement planning system . . . a system that is both urgently needed and long overdue!"

Sample Connector

"But, unless we move quickly, we can 'drop the ball' . . . for this type of system requires careful planning and design and could take months to complete. It's challenging . . . but we can do it!"

Sample Selection from Main Body

"So . . . the key supports for this system would be in the startup of weekly information seminars, where everyone over 55 would be invited. Note that these programs would be given over the lunchtime hour, so as to create a casual, informative atmosphere, yet not reduce productivity."

Sample Power Close

"Also, besides the other action steps needed, in order to have this type of system, we must start moving immediately! As a first item, we need 10 volunteers from this group to be part of a steering committee to guide this project all the way through—all that's required is two hours a week for the next six to eight weeks.

"By volunteering, you will be doing our company and yourselves a real service . . . not bad, for just a few hours a week! Now, let's see your hands held high!"

Speaker Tips:

- Use handouts which summarize the main elements, features and benefits of the early retirement planning system.
- Try to include as many do-it-yourself worksheets as possible.
- Always include the name(s) and address of people who are available to answer questions after the presentation is over (include a several-month time period here.
- Never claim to be the "ultimate authority" when questions arise. If you don't know the answer, say so! But find out, and later on get back to the person who raised it.
- Never lose patience with what you perceive as a simplistic or basic question (even if its brought up in several variations) remember that the subject matter affects people's egos, sense of worth and self-esteem.

Sample Questions

Here is a list of typical questions that might be raised at the conclusion of a presentation on early retirement planning.

1. Why is there a need for this type of planning?
2. Does the company have a "hidden motive" in presenting this?
3. How does early retirement planning fit in with the recently revised tax laws?
4. How many employees could be affected by this?
5. Is the program mandatory? What if an employee is offered it, and turns it down?
6. How much is the program going to cost?
7. How will our stockholders be notified of this? Any chance of their having an adverse reaction?
8. Does this program replace or supplement the current social security program?
9. What is the minimum age requirement for eligibility for early retirement?
10. Does this now mean that a person *cannot* work past their 65th birthday?

Chapter Summary

You have now completed Chapter 7 which illustrated how presentations in four typical business categories can be successfully presented before a live audience.

Each of these examples were specifically chosen for two reasons. To begin with, all of them are topics quite common in today's world of business. Secondly, they are diversified enough to represent a broad spectrum of topics that are used in business presentations throughout the world. By working through each example, you now should be reasonably prepared to start work on *your* next presentation.

Now you are ready to begin Part Two of Business Presentation Techniques . . . a special section devoted to additional techniques that can be used to enhance *any* talk. Let's begin with tips from the "pros" on making your next presentation even better!

Memory Joggers

☑ When the primary purpose of your talk is *to inform*, the major emphasis would usually focus on the following:

- Keeping the presentation factual (but still interesting)
- Trying for early audience attention, then continuing to build interest
- Retaining a crisp quality through effective pacing and voice modulation
- Heavy use of audiovisual

- Liberal use of WIFMs and benefits
- Being as factual as possible
- Using handouts where appropriate

☑ Conversely, avoid,

- Thinking that everyone will be in full agreement with the points you are making
- Using humor (unless you are absolutely certain of its value)
- Showing favoritism, or taking sides with any issue (be as impartial as possible).
- Displaying any type of impatience with questions raised by the audience.

☑ When your talk falls under the other two categories of the strategies classification chart (i.e., to motivate or persuade), the same elements of what to focus on, and conversely, what to avoid) would essentially be the same. The difference (additions or deletions from the above list) would be based on the rule of common sense—using appropriate speaking strategy and tactics that would compliment your presentation and the audience listening to it.

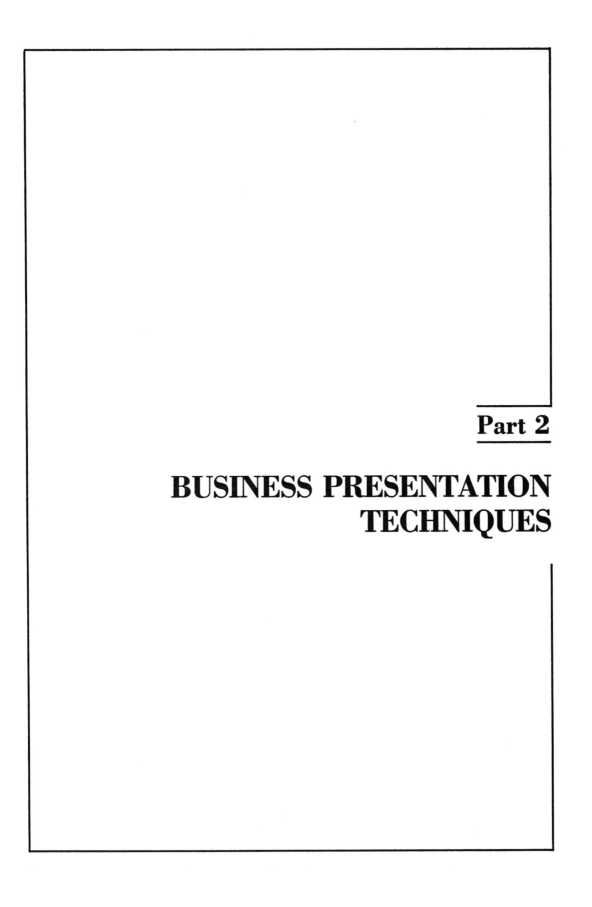

Part 2

BUSINESS PRESENTATION TECHNIQUES

CHAPTER 8

Tips on Improving Your Presentation Techniques

This chapter focuses on key techniques used by professional speakers to enhance their presentations. You'll find information on how to "warm up" your audience and establish rapport, how to reduce anxiety and minimize tension, and four reasons why a presentation can fail—and what you can do to prevent it.

The Warm-Up Technique

This is a simple but highly effective time-tested strategy that you can employ immediately. It involves meeting with participants just prior to your talk. For example, let's assume that your presentation is scheduled for 9:00 A.M. The people who will be attending are not familiar with you. You learn that coffee and Danish will be served to the audience beginning at 8:15 A.M. You arrive shortly after 8:15 and make it a point to meet as many attendees as possible.

Speaker Tips:

The more people you meet in advance, the easier it will be to establish and maintain rapport with them during your talk.

Three Benefits of Repeating a Person's Name When Introduced to Him

You can add three important benefits to your warm-up by remembering to repeat aloud each participant's name as you are greeting or being introduced to them:

1. You will flatter the participant by having his or her name mentioned in this way. It shows you care about the person.

2. This technique offers a strong memory reinforcer to you, particularly if you want to call on a participant by name or speak with him or her after the presentation.

3. The simple act of greeting people prior to your presentation can usually help relax you to a marked degree. In effect, by following this procedure, you are now talking to a group of new-found friends instead of strangers.

Here's an example of a speaker using this technique in a relaxed, informal manner . . .

Speaker:

"Good morning . . . don't believe we have met. My name is Frank Stanton, and I'll be your speaker this morning."

Participant:

"Nice to meet you Mr. Stanton. I'm Marilyn Sachs from the Detroit office."

Speaker:

"Pleasure to meet you <u>Marilyn</u>. By any chance would you be the same Marilyn Sachs who was featured in last month's company newsletter—as the winner of the midwest service excellence award?"

Participant:

"Well . . . yes. Didn't think the people in the other regions read about us!"

Speaker:

"Sure we do, Marilyn. As a matter of fact, this is just another example of how communication can be improved in our company. I plan to address this point during my talk, and would be interested in hearing your reaction afterwards."

Speaker Tips:

By talking with participants before your talk, you can pick up important information that can be used during the introduction of your presentation. For example, suppose you met nine people, all of whom had to fly or drive to the presentation, with an average trip taking five hours. Using this as your "bridge," you could weave in comments like:

- *"Seems like the typical person I met over coffee this morning had to travel more than five hours to get here. This only proves to me that*

Speaker Tips (continued):

> *you have high expectations about this presentation ... and I don't*
> *intend to let you down."*
>
> or
>
> • *"Due to the poor weather last night, I learned that three of the partic-*
> *ipants had to spend most of the night in their local airport, waiting*
> *out the fog in order to arrive here on time. That's a pretty high price*
> *to pay to hear <u>anyone</u> speak! Now that you are all here, I'll do my*
> *best to make <u>your trip</u> well worth it!"*

How to Reduce Anxiety Levels

Nine Easy Steps to Controlling Pretalk Jitters

High levels of anxiety will usually trigger a corresponding rise in tension within the speaker—a condition to be avoided, or at least reduced as much as possible, by everyone who hopes to deliver a professional presentation. Left unchecked, it will increase the risk of actually delivering a poor or marginal talk, and foster the feeling of self-doubt.

There is a high correlation between the range of negativism in the perceived attitude and the degree of probable success. In other words, the self-doubt syndrome portrays a classic example of the self-fulfilling prophecy, where the prediction of eventual success or failure is directly linked to that person's expectations.

> **Speaker Tips:**
>
> If you perceive that you *will* succeed as a professional speaker, chances are good that you will achieve that goal. However, the reverse can also hold true.

As a starter, it's important to realize that a small degree of tension is quite normal, and in fact, desirable. Small pools of tension in a person just prior to the talk keeps the speaker at the maximum efficiency level and highly alert to both the room environment and audience mood. However, when these levels of pretalk jitters become unusually high, the results can reverse themselves rather quickly, and an unproductive situation will often result.

Figure 8-1 illustrates a nine-step method that has shown a high success rate for a wide range of business presentations. The steps are designed to help you relax before your talk. Some benefits of the nine-step model are:

• The exercise can be done quietly, without drawing attention to yourself.

- The exercise can be timed, so as to complete the nine steps just prior to beginning your presentation.
- If necessary, the exercise can be interrupted and resumed later, with no loss of efficiency.

Speaker Tips:

Don't be discouraged if the pretalk relaxation technique described in Figure 8-1 seems cumbersome or doesn't work the first time it is attempted. Keep practicing. It may take a while to feel the results, but your patience will be rewarded and you will be a more effective speaker.

How to Use the SFETS Method to Help Minimize Tension

How tense you are before your presentation will depend to some extent on your expertise in giving a talk. Fortunately, for most presenters, the anxiety level experienced just prior to a talk rapidly begins to disappear as the talk progresses.

For those less fortunate speakers who do not normally benefit from this automatic lessening of tension, additional help is needed. The SFETS relaxation technique (illustrated in Figure 8-2) is an invaluable aid, not only to the novice presenter, but to speakers of any experience level.

SFETS is an acronym that stands for the following:

S: Sweep the room with your eyes.

F: Focus on one person.

E: Eye contact should be maintained.

T: Talk in a measured pace.

S: Sweep and focus again.

Let's look at each of these steps more closely.

You begin by *sweeping* the parameter of the entire room with your eyes, first to one side and then to the other. From the audience's viewpoint, this gives the speaker a sense of authority and command, and helps to heighten interest.

Next, you begin *focusing* on one person in the audience who appears to be receptive to your forthcoming presentation. This helps relax you; you will have a direct visual contact with a member of the audience. It also helps maintain the audience's attention.

Maintain the established *eye contact* until you have assembled your initial opening thoughts. This short pause will take only a few seconds, but it will further increase interest in what you are about to say.

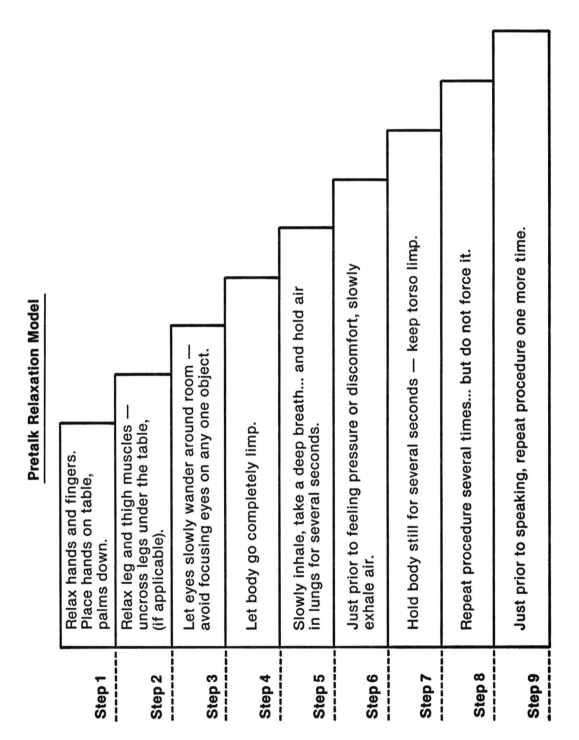

Pretalk Relaxation Model

Step 1 — Relax hands and fingers. Place hands on table, palms down.

Step 2 — Relax leg and thigh muscles — uncross legs under the table, (if applicable).

Step 3 — Let eyes slowly wander around room — avoid focusing eyes on any one object.

Step 4 — Let body go completely limp.

Step 5 — Slowly inhale, take a deep breath... and hold air in lungs for several seconds.

Step 6 — Just prior to feeling pressure or discomfort, slowly exhale air.

Step 7 — Hold body still for several seconds — keep torso limp.

Step 8 — Repeat procedure several times... but do not force it.

Step 9 — Just prior to speaking, repeat procedure one more time.

FIGURE 8-1:
Pretalk Relaxation Model

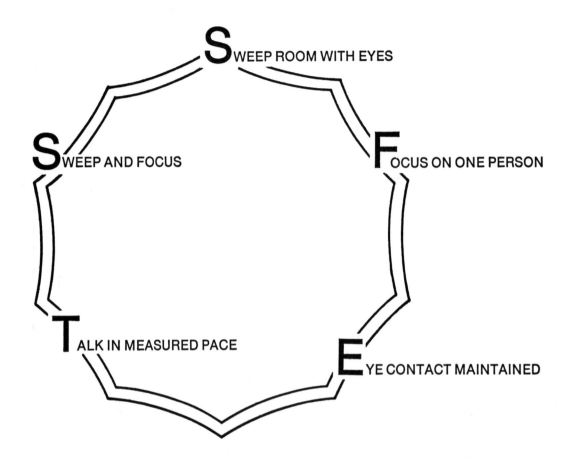

FIGURE 8-2:
The SFETS Method for Relaxation

Begin *talking at a controlled pace*. This helps to set the overall mood of the presentation and to get things started on the right track. Many speakers inadvertently talk at too rapid a rate, which is a sure sign of nervousness.

Continue *sweeping* the audience with your eyes, occasionally stopping to *focus* on one person. This will give you an added sense of presence as a speaker and help you build rapport with your audience.

Speaker Tips:

The use of a carefully measured pause is a highly effective attention-getting device.

How the "Pros" Prepare Presentation Notes

Regardless of the type of business presentation to be given, the inexperienced speaker stands a good chance of inadvertently developing a set of notes that not only will not enhance the forthcoming talk, but in many cases will actually detract from the presentation. Falling into this trap by no means implies that the speaker has not done enough research or preparation for the forthcoming talk. Although every case is different, *the main problem seems to be in the ability to translate what one has to say into a workable format for use on the platform.* Let's review some of the problems that can be encountered.

Four Reasons Why a Presentation Can Fail

- Using a well-meaning, but endless assortment of notes in various forms of shorthand on scraps of paper.
- Writing out the text of the speech on 8½" × 11½" paper where every word to be delivered has been carefully spelled out.
- Using various compilations of shorthand for key points you want to make in no special format or planned delivery sequence.
- Using a variety of other assorted strategies and well-meaning plans that somehow never really aid the speaker in converting what has to be said into a simplified guide for actually saying it.

Three Steps to a Better Presentation

Professional speakers have discovered a simplified guide for condensing both main and supporting statements into a sequential pattern. They place these notes directly onto standard 3" × 5" index cards. *Proper use of this one effective speaking technique will significantly enhance your skills during a business presentation.* The format is based on a simple three-step process that can be learned in just a few minutes:

Step One: Review existing material for the forthcoming talk, then write out the main substance in paragraph form.

Step Two: Review each paragraph and mark up words into main points for conversational phrases and emphasis where necessary.

Step Three: Rewrite each main point into a sequential outline, using subheadings where necessary. Highlight key words or phrases.

The following is a simplified example of how the three steps could be used in actual practice (for illustrative purposes, only the first two paragraphs of the talk will be shown).

Step One (Write main substance in paragraph form.)
   Our new product development strategy will now take on a highly focused market ap-

*proach. During the past several years, although the majority of our new production intro-
ductions were generally considered satisfactory, none were ever outstanding in terms of either unit sales or bottom line profitability During the past five-year period, we never
captured more then 4.5 percent of total market share, although our advertising budget has
increased by a minimum of 5 percent each year.*

*We intend to start reversing that trend right now. During the next few weeks, we will
be announcing our new Model XB100, 18-inch hedge trimmer designed specifically for the
first-time homeowner. Keeping our market research highly centered on our target customer
base, we found that approximately 35 percent of this type of hedge clipper was purchased as
gifts (rather than bought directly by the user). Further, almost 65 percent of these units were
sold in the discount-type department and specialty stores. Although price is a definite factor
in purchase psychology, both quality and reliability are strong buying decision influencers.
The new XB100 has been specifically designed to capture a greater share of this market!*

Step Two (Separate words into phrases emphasizing main points.)

*Our new product development strategy/will now take on a highly focused market
approach./During the past several years,/although the majority of our new product introductions were generally considered satisfactory,/none were ever outstanding/in terms of either unit sales or bottom line profitability./During the past five-year period,/we never captured more than 4.5 percent of total market share,/although our advertising budget has
increased/by a minimum of 5 percent each year.*

*We intend to start reversing that trend right now./During the next few weeks, we will
be announcing our new model XB100,/18-inch hedge trimmer/designed specifically for the
first-time homeowner./Keeping our market research highly centered on our target customer
base, we found that approximately 35 percent of this type of hedge clipper was purchased as
gifts/(rather than bought directly by the user). Further, almost 65 percent of these units
were sold in the discount-type department and specialty stores./Although price is a definite
factor/in purchase psychology, both quality and reliability/are strong buying decision influencers./The new XB100 has been specifically designed to capture a greater share of this
market!*

Step Three (Rewrite main emphasis points into a tight outline)

New Product Development Strategy

- Revised heavily to focus on market
- Previous product intro's never outstanding
- Marginal results in unit sales/profitability
- Although budgets increased yearly, we never captured more than 4.5 per-
cent of market share

Model XB100, 18-Inch Hedge Trimmer

- Designed specifically for target market and greater sales penetration
- 35 percent of product type purchased as gifts

NEW PRODUCT DEVELOPMENT STRATEGY

- REVISED HEAVILY TO FOCUS ON MARKET
- PREVIOUS PRODUCT INTRO'S NEVER OUTSTANDING
- MARGINAL RESULTS IN UNIT SALES/PROFITABILITY
- ALTHOUGH BUDGETS INCREASED YEARLY, WE NEVER CAPTURED MORE THAN 4.5% OF MARKET SHARE

MODEL XB100 ~ 18 INCH HEDGE TRIMMER

- DESIGNED SPECIFICALLY FOR TARGET MARKET AND GREATER SALES PENETRATION
- 35% OF PRODUCT TYPE PURCHASED AS GIFTS
- 65% SOLD PRIMARILY IN DISCOUNT TYPE STORES
- QUALITY AND RELIABILITY MORE IMPORTANT THAN PRICE TO CONSUMER
- OUR FIRST PRODUCT DESIGNED TO REVERSE MEDIOCRE COMPANY SALES PERFORMANCE — AND MAKE US INDUSTRY LEADER!

FIGURE 8-3:
Index Card Format for Preparing Notes

Putting the Three Steps to Use

This work page offers you a chance to practice the three-step process for a successful summary format.

1. Glance over the first few paragraphs of a presentation you plan to give. Write out the first three or four paragraphs in the space provided below.
2. Go back and separate the sentences you just wrote into main points for conversational phrases and emphasis. Use diagonal lines to help differentiate.
3. Now rewrite the main headings and emphasis points in a tight outline.

Heading: _____

Emphasis Points:
- _____
- _____
- _____
- _____

Heading: _____

Emphasis Points:
- _____
- _____
- _____
- _____

Heading: _____

Emphasis Points:
- _____
- _____
- _____
- _____

- 65 percent sold primarily in discount-type stores
- Quality and reliability more important than price to consumer
- Our first product designed to reverse mediocre company sales performance—and make us an industry leader!

Now . . . compare the original two paragraphs listed in Step One with the tightened-up outline versions as shown in Step Three. Notice how much more concise and easy to read the revised formats have become, in spite of the fact that I have taken some liberty in translating the text into a more concise form! In other words, it is *not* necessary to strive for exact duplications of wording from one step to the next. As long as Step Three contains the *essential elements* of your presentation in concise form, you are well on the way to a more effective talk.

Figure 8-3 displays how the first two paragraphs would appear on separate index cards via a person's handwriting. All things being equal, to make each point as clear as possible, it would be preferable to have these notes typewritten, but it's not necessary, as long as your handwriting is reasonably legible! It is also acceptable to use a larger size index card. The advantage here is that it would hold more words than a 3″ × 5″ version. On the other hand, they are a bit more difficult to handle on the platform due to their size.

One of the major benefits here is that once the three-step technique is mastered, it can be used *independently* via the index cards, or incorporated into a comprehensive (yet, easy to use) all-in-one system designed to make each presentation more professional than the next.

Twelve Ways to Enhance Your Next Business Presentation

Most business presentations generally are given in front of a captive audience whose time is usually limited. Accordingly:

1. Keep every presentation as short as possible. Experience has shown that most talks can be cut by as much as 25 percent, without losing any significant value.
2. If you are not familiar with the audience, make every effort beforehand to learn of their backgrounds and (if possible), expectations. Always keep in mind that several people in the room may know more about the subject than you do!
3. *Never* take any audience for granted. Even if you have given the talk 100 times before, make certain that the presentation retains its original crispness.
4. Use audiovisual aids wherever possible . . . *especially* in a business presentation on a technical or difficult subject.

5. Respect the audience's time. If the talk is scheduled to go on at 9:00 AM, that's when it should start. Otherwise, you do a disservice to those who did arrive on time, and are kept waiting for "others to arrive".

6. As a courtesy to the group, early on in the presentation, mention appropriately how long you plan to talk, and when questions will be answered.

7. When you don't know the answer to a specific question, admit it. The typical business audience does not expect you to know everything, and they will respect you more for it. However, if you promise to get back to someone with the answer at a later date, remember to do just that!

8. Always dress for the occasion. Try not to "overdress" or (correspondingly) appear too casual. If you have to err, it's far better to be slightly overdressed.

9. Always remember to keep your words as simple as possible. Long-winded words and phrases don't impress an audience . . . it usually confuses them.

10. Restrict the use of humor unless you are confident that it is appropriate, not offensive to anyone in the room, and you are sure of the timing.

11. Where possible, try to distribute handouts at the *end* of your talk, not *during*. (It provides a great "crutch" for really busy people, who might consider your handout as a summary . . . and pay less attention to what you are saying. Worse yet, they may even feel confident enough to leave early!)

12. And, if you remember nothing else, keep in mind the three tested rules for a really professional presentation . . . Practice, practice, then practice some more!

Chapter Summary

You have now successfully completed the study of Chapter 8 which outlined specific tips on improving your presentation techniques. This included the warm-up method, several ways to reduce anxiety levels just prior to the talk, and the technique of preparing presentation notes for a more effective talk in front of any business group.

Now you are ready to start work on the interpretation and application of body language . . . those nonverbal clues which have a significant impact on each and every talk that you give.

Memory Joggers

☑ When speaking to a group who doesn't know you, arrive early and try to meet as many of the audience members as possible prior to your presentation.

☑ Practice the pretalk relaxation technique a few minutes each night at home before attempting it in front of a live audience.

☑ Regardless of the size of your audience, remember to establish eye contact with one person in the center of the room until your presentation is well underway.

☑ Use the SFETS technique to help minimize tension: Sweep the room with your eyes, Focus on one person, keep Eye contact maintained, Talk in a measured pace, and continue to Sweep and focus periodically.

☑ Don't try to memorize your entire speech or write it out word for word on paper. Index cards, summarizing the key points you wish to make, are more effective and less cumbersome.

CHAPTER 9

Body Language: How Your Actions Affect Your Words

This chapter will help you identify successful presentation trait clusters used by professionals. You will learn how you can exhibit some of these skills in your next presentation, *without* changing your personality or style of delivery. Highlighting the individual skill areas requiring correction, then applying a systematic follow-up, will put you well ahead on the road to a more effective presentation.

How Professional Role Models Can Help Your Performance

One of the most valuable aids in developing a more effective business presentation is to first identify those professionals in the field who are clearly outstanding in their use of this skill.

The object here is *not* to attempt to emulate personal characteristics or individual style. This will not work, for the simple reason that each of us has his or her own unique delivery style, and striving to copy someone else's personality in front of a group will result in a mismatch, and lead to a less than satisfactory talk.

What *is* required, however, is to identify the common traits exhibited by these top speakers—techniques they use which help their presentations to be truly outstanding. Honing in on these *traits*, not the speakers' personalities, will be a positive force in your quest for better business presentations.

155

How to Identify 11 Key Presentation Traits Found in Successful Speakers

There are 11 traits exhibited by most professional speakers:

1. Strong presence
2. Audience empathy
3. Use of an effective opening
4. Good eye contact
5. Sincerity
6. Enthusiasm
7. Effective gestures for emphasis
8. No apparent nervousness
9. Good voice control
10. Appropriate dress
11. Persuasive close

Of course, no list of this type could be all-inclusive, but it does offer the most popular traits found in successful speakers.

Form 3 lists these 11 traits and leaves room for you to fill in additional traits as you may wish. A filled-in sample of this form is shown in Figure 9-1. Clarifying these traits in other people is relatively easy. As a starter, most of these traits become more obvious when you observe the person in action. On the other hand, many of these pleasing characteristics can be found each night on television. For example, the next time you watch television, take a cross-cut sampling of television personalities. It would probably be no surprise to find the results seen in Figure 9-1.

Naturally, each of the television personalities listed could easily spill into another trait, but the point remains that the traits can be readily identified by the observer.

A final point is worth noting here. Over the years, many people have asked me which of these trait clusters are the most important. I always respond that they are *all* important—some perhaps more than others, at a given moment in time—depending on the nature of the talk.

Speaker Tips:

Although it's preferable to list the names of people you know personally when completing Form 3, you can also list the names of well-known personalities or public figures.

Let's briefly review each of the 11 traits and describe what they mean in the real world of public speaking.

EFFECTIVE PRESENTATION TRAITS

TRAIT	ROLE MODEL	HOW EXHIBITED
Strong presence	President Ronald Reagan	Dominating personality, assumes natural air of command
Audience empathy	Phil Donahue (TV talkshow host)	Relates easily to everyone in a convincing way
An effective opening	Senator Edward Kennedy	Generally, has good WIFMs in talk opening
Good eye contact	Reverend Jesse Jackson	Effective eye sweep of room, zeros in on one person
Sincerity	Pope John Paul	Effective use of words, pauses, body language and eye contact
Enthusiasm	Jerry Lewis (comedian)	Energetic body language, short WIFMs and constant motion
Effective gestures	Pope John Paul	Excellent use of arms and overall non-verbal language
No apparent nervousness	Mikhail Gorbachev	No fumbling, shyness; correct posture, erect, straightforward
Good voice control	Dolly Parton (singer)	Never squeaky, nice use of pauses, well modulated tone control
Appropriate dress	Nancy Reagan	Outfit always appropriate for the occasion, night or day
Persuasive close	Dan Rather (CBS newsman)	Always well connected to entire talk and flows naturally

FIGURE 9-1:
Effective Presentation Traits (Filled-in Sample of Form 3)

TRAIT	T.V. ANCHORPERSON (PRIME-TIME VIEWING)	QUIZ-SHOW M.C.	LEADING ACTOR T.V. SERIES
Strong Presence	✔	✔	✔
Audience Empathy		✔	
An Effective Opening	✔	✔	
Good Eye Contact	✔		✔
Sincerity	✔	✔	
Enthusiasm		✔	
Effective Gestures	✔	✔	✔
No Apparent Nervousness	✔	✔	✔
Good Voice Control	✔		✔
Appropriate Dress	✔	✔	✔

1. *Strong presence:* The presenter easily relates to the needs and desires of those listening to his or her words. Not only is this done quite naturally by the speaker, but the effect is one of creating interest and solidarity from the audience as a whole. The speaker easily commands the respect of the audience with a natural combination of flair, poise, authority, and a delicate sense of timing.

2. *Audience empathy:* For whatever reason, you couldn't help but like the speaker. From the very first words spoken, the presenter seemed to form a natural, close bond with the audience. It made people relax more, feeling that they were more in the company of a trusted friend, rather than someone they had never heard speak before. And (the most amazing part of all) this empathy with the audience appeared to develop in a low-keyed natural manner.

3. *An effective opening:* While you may not remember specifically what was said, you can easily recall that it immediately caught your attention and left you wanting to hear more. This feeling stays with you throughout the entire presentation.

4. *Good eye contact:* The speaker's eyes seemed to shift from one side of the room to the other in an unhurried, carefully paced pattern. During several points in the talk, you were certain that he was looking specifically at you. Naturally, when this occurred, you paid even greater attention to what was being said. Interestingly enough, you got the distinct impression that others in the audience had the same impression.

5. *Sincerity:* From the moment the talk began, you sensed a deep sincerity on the part of the speaker. This genuine commitment to the topic seemed to permeate the room and, in turn, helped to foster a strong bond between the audience and presenter. A genuine honesty seemed to exude from the speaker throughout the entire presentation.

6. *Enthusiasm:* The high level of enthusiasm generated by the speaker rapidly became contagious throughout the room. This action not only raised your own excitement level, but made you want to listen attentively to everything that was being said.

7. *Effective gestures:* All body gestures made by the presenter appeared to enhance the talk greatly. These included use of hands, facial gestures, and the occasional shifting of the body itself to reinforce the point being made at that moment.

8. *No apparent nervousness:* Not only didn't the speaker appear nervous, he actually seemed to be enjoying himself throughout the entire talk! Of all the successful speaking traits shown by professional speakers, this probably left the deepest impression upon you. In fact, this trait is invariably found in every successful speaker.

9. *Good voice control:* You were aware that the presenter's voice had a very pleasant tone throughout the talk. The occasional use of pauses, careful voice modulation, and deliberate pacing seemed to blend perfectly with the presentation . . . and appeared quite natural.

10. *Appropriate dress:* The speaker's clothing appeared to reinforce what the speaker's message was, yet nothing the speaker wore distracted from the presentation being made.

Speaker Tips:

Guidelines for Appropriate Dress

Common sense in what to wear should always apply. In general, most professional speakers will dress for the occasion, not the audience. Thus, a vice-president of manufacturing, who normally wears a three-piece suit, upon speaking to a group of first-line supervisors who are wearing casual clothes in an assembly area, should **not** wear a sport shirt. He should wear his regular business attire.

      Men: Avoid light colored clothing. It's generally safe to wear a medium dark blue, gray, or brown suit. A blue shirt and conservative tie are a safe combination.

Women: Try to steer away from a very casual look. It's usually acceptable to wear a medium dark, solid color dress, or a tailored suit with a complimentary blouse. Stay away from flashy jewelry or anything that "jingles" (like several rows of bracelets).

---

11. *Persuasive close:* The close was introduced as smoothly and as effectively as the opening. At the conclusion of the talk, you remembered not only what the speaker had said, but also felt a high degree of commitment to those points that were made.

Eight Body Language Signals to Avoid

1. Arms clasped or folded tightly around chest (makes you appear unsure and defensive)
2. Drumming fingers on podium (highly distracting to audience)
3. Slumped shoulders during presentation . . . or slouching (carries the appearance of defeat)
4. Inadvertent tugging at ear or jingling coins in pocket (confuses/distracts people listening to your talk)
5. Keeping a tight grip on podium "until knuckles turn white" (a sure sign that you are in deep fear/distress!)
6. Constantly pointing finger at audience to make a point (OK used sparingly—any more appears dictatorial)
7. Heavy use of pauses . . . "the overkill" (used in moderation a pause is quite effective . . . too many destroys the talk)
8. Frequent pacing around speaker's podium (will greatly distract audience from the point you are trying to get across)

Clue	*Interpretation*
Poor eye contact	Shyness and possible insecurity
Taking off glasses, and pausing before making major point	An important point is being made by the speaker
Clenched fists during talk	Hostility, which could be a reaction to insecurity on platform
Heavy pacing around podium or on platform	Apparent nervousness, ill-at-ease
Constantly tugging at tie or collar	An outlet for uneasiness being experienced by speaker
Frequent clearing of throat	Unless a medical problem, caused by simple nervousness
Constant staring at one (or more) person(s) in audience	Exhibiting dominance (or possibly hostility)
Tapping of pen or pencil on podium	Difficult to pinpoint exact cause—could stem from nervousness, impatience or could be an outlet for anger/resentment

Interpretation of Nonverbal Signs

While there is no uniform consensus from the experts, the majority generally agrees on the meaning of the following nonverbal clues.

Speaker Tips:

- Remember that most of the meaning of your words is conveyed not by what you say, but by how you looked when you said it!
- While **all** presentation traits are important, in order to have a really professional talk you must have the following: a strong presence on the platform, good eye contact, and no apparent nervousness.

Checklist of Appropriate Skills for Follow-Up

Now that you have finished the review of effective presentation trait skills, you should be in a position to finalize a *checklist of appropriate skills for follow-up*. The purpose of this is to highlight areas which still require improvement into categories of the effective presentation trait clusters used successfully by professional speakers.

To assist you in this effort, let's look at Figure 9-2. Note that it has been especially designed so you can use the form yourself—deciding areas (a) where you may need to improve (b) where you have a satisfactory level of competence, and (c) where you are not certain.

Here we see the form in action, showing that (based upon the talk given on January 19th and 25th), the speaker merely checked the three applicable categories to be used as a base for follow-up during the next talk. Note however, that the checklist was completed only three days after the second talk . . . while all details were fresh in the speaker's mind. This is an important point. Finally, (as shown on the form in the enthusiasm category), if a trait falls somewhere in between two categories, merely connect the checkmarks.

As future presentations are made, the checklist can be modified accordingly.

Figure 9-3 shows a partially completed sample of Form 5 used as a follow-up to the previous talks given on January 19th and 25th (Figure 9-3). Let's take a closer look at how the speaker was able to specifically improve selected areas of previous presentations through a "self-help" method.

1. Based on the talks of the 19th and 25th, the speaker listed four areas requiring improvement. They were

CHECKLIST OF APPROPRIATE SKILLS FOR FOLLOW UP

Date talk(s) given ___1/19/88___
___1/25/88___

Date checklist completed ___1/28/88___

Trait/Skill	I need to improve	I perform satisfactorily	Not certain
Strong presence		✓	
Audience empathy		✓	
Effective opening	✓		
Good eye contact		✓	
Sincerity		✓	
Enthusiasm		✓	✓
Effective gestures	✓		
Nervousness	✓		
Voice control		✓	
Appropriate dress		✓	
Persuasive close		✓	

FIGURE 9-2:
Checklist of Appropriate Skills for Follow-Up (Filled-in sample of Form 4)

FOLLOW-UP ACTION GUIDE

Skill Areas Requiring Correction	Remedial Action to be Taken During			Date / Results Obtained
	Talk #1 Date: 2/2	Talk #2 Date: 2/18	Talk #3 Date: TBD	
Effective opening	✓			2/2/28. Good use of WIIFMs. Much improvement noted. Helped my ego.
Enthusiasm	✓	✓		2/18/88. Still a bit "low-key!" More improvement needed. Will try on next talk.
Effective gestures		✓		2/18/88. Much better use of body language. Will continue to practice skill.
Nervousness			✓	

FIGURE 9-3:
Follow-up Action Guide (Filled-in Sample of Form 5)

- Effective opening
- Enthusiasm
- Effective gestures
- Nervousness

2. Knowing that two additional presentations were scheduled on February 2nd and February 18th, the speaker decided to concentrate on the *effective opening* and *higher enthusiasm* level for the talk on February 2nd. The attempt for more *effective gestures* was preserved for the presentation on February 18th. Since the area of *nervousness* on the platform remained a steadily improving (but still not quite satisfactory) situation, the presenter decided to hold off on this until the third talk (which he knew was to be scheduled in late February).

3. Note in the date/results obtained column, that the talk on February 2nd resulted in a much more effective opening—while the level of enthusiasm still needed more work. Conversely, the talk on February 18th resulted in more effective gestures.

4. During talk three, while the speaker would concentrate mainly on nervousness, he would still try to improve the level of enthusiasm.

Chapter Summary

You have now completed work on Chapter 9, which described how your actions affect your words during a business presentation. You learned 11 key presentation traits that are used by successful speakers, and were introduced to two checklists for appropriate follow-up skills and action.

As you now can see, one of the fundamental steps in becoming more proficient as a speaker is to determine your current deficient skill areas in front of an audience. This chapter enabled you to compare those below-par skills against skills demonstrated by the pros—with specific guides for self-improvement.

You are now in a position to begin work on how to use audiovisual aids to enhance our next presentation.

Memory Joggers

☑ No two speakers are exactly alike. Each of us has our own unique delivery presence.

☑ Selecting a role model will help you identify common trait clusters you may wish to emulate.

☑ "Audience empathy" means that the presenter relates easily to the needs and desires of those listening to his words.

☑ An effective opening is one that immediately catches your attention.

☑ Effective gestures include careful hand and facial gestures as well as the occasional shifting of your body.

CHAPTER 10

How to Use Audiovisual Aids to Enhance Your Presentation

Business presentations can be greatly enhanced by the use of audiovisual aids. This chapter focuses on the leading types of aids available, and the most efficient ways in which they can be used. Special emphasis is given to both the advantages and disadvantages of each category.

Two points should be kept in mind when reading this chapter. First, even if you were *never* to use a slide, video, overhead projector, or flipchart, you would still have audiovisual play a part of your presentation, because verbal and non-verbal mannerisms (as discussed in Chapter 9) are an audiovisual medium unto themselves.

Second, while this chapter does focus on the advantages and disadvantages of different audiovisual aids, it does not include technical information on the specific preparation of slides, how to use various kinds of projection equipment, or the care and maintenance of film and hardware. All of these techniques are usually covered in detail in the instructional/maintenance booklets included with each piece of equipment, or you could find similar information from audiovisual dealers.

The Flipchart or Standing Easel

This is one of the most common and simplest visual aids employed today. Combining both ease of use and trouble-free operation, the flipchart has become one of the most frequently used aids to presenters around the world.

Advantages

- Very portable (paper can be separated from the easel or carried with the folded stand)
- Highly flexible in both ease of operation and where "last minute" changes are required
- With use of "tabbing" (coding each page with a strip of masking tape to identify a page heading) the presenter is *not* restricted to page sequencing, but has the ability of random access when required
- Can be quite effective visually when used in close distances to the audience (generally, this effect is lost when audiences are more than twenty to thirty feet away from the flipchart)

Disadvantages

- Generally, all flipcharts should be prepared in advance
- A definite "stand alone" aid (as compared to combining both visual and auditory effects in a sound/slide presentation)
- Audience must be relatively close to the flipchart for maximum effect

The Blackboard

Like the flipchart, the blackboard is one of the simplest visual aids in use, although not being used as much as in years past.

Advantages

- Usually portable (where blackboard frame is mounted on rollers)
- Quite easy to use
- Since the area surface of a blackboard is generally larger than a flipchart, it can be seen from a greater distance
- Trouble-free operation

Disadvantages

- More cumbersome to work with than a flipchart
- Using chalk can be messy
- Generally restricted to using one color
- Board must be washed after each use

35 Millimeter Slides

As a general rule, slides are relatively inexpensive to prepare, easy to use in the presentation and offer the speaker a wide degree of flexibility. Let's take a closer look at some of the "pros" and "cons" involved.

Advantages

- Compatible with a wide variety and type of slide projectors (regardless of projector voltage requirements)
- Generally, never a bulk or storage problem when stored either in boxes or slide trays
- Content of presentation can be easily changed or modified at a later date (especially important in business presentations where a "last minute" change in facts or figures can easily occur)
- Slides are very portable, and where necessary, can easily be mailed to another location or carried by the speaker
- Can be either cardboard or glass mounted, depending upon requirements
- Easily duplicated to provide for a "spare set" or when multiple copies are required
- Frees the speaker from heavy reliance on prepared notes
- Where desired, can be easily converted to videotape or overhead transparencies

Disadvantages

- Always the danger of "slide overloading" (or attempting to cram too much information on the slide)
- On certain occasions, slides may require (or be greatly enhanced by) an audio-track
- Slides are not indestructible. They require periodic cleaning to keep them in good operating condition
- 35mm slides can easily get worn with frequent use (e.g., such as the cardboard mount becoming frayed or bent)
- When being loaded into trays, slides must always be numbered and put into proper sequencing. Let's not forget, that unless double-checked, slides can easily be inserted upside-down or reversed in the tray
- In certain cases, room must be fairly dark to insure good audience visibility

Overhead Projector

The overhead projector is, perhaps one of the most common types of hardware in use today, due to its wide availability and simplicity of operation. It is used mainly with two types of transparencies:

1. The *prepared version*, which is either completed in advance by the presenter, or prepared commercially through an outside source.
2. The *"Do-It-Yourself"* type which is accomplished through writing on

single blank acetate sheets (either before or during the actual presentation) or drawing on a supplied acetate roll attached to the projector.

Advantages
- Usually very reliable to operate—even over extended periods of time
- In most cases, easy to transport from one location to another
- Widely available as a rental through audiovisual dealers
- Very simple to operate
- Usually, room lights do not have to be drastically dimmed
- Transparencies can be quickly prepared for projector use

Disadvantages
- Some projectors can be bulky to carry
- Overhead projector transparencies can be difficult to store (due to their relatively large size as compared to 35mm slides)
- Care always must be taken not to overheat projector; otherwise damage to the motor or transparencies can easily occur

16 Millimeter Film

As both an alternate and (in many cases) a successor to 8mm film, it allows the presenter a wide variety of visual effects, plus flexibility in content and usage.

Advantages
- When used properly, generally creates (and holds) audience interest
- Films can either be created "in-house" or professionally done
- Usually provides a high degree of realism
- When produced correctly, provides clear expression of thoughts and ideas in fluid motion
- Where desired, film can be converted to videotape to increase flexibility of use

Disadvantages
- Although highly desirable, customized productions from outside producers are usually expensive
- Films can become outdated very quickly

- If not stored properly (insulated from heat, direct sun or high humidity), film can deteriorate very rapidly
- It is often difficult to obtain a professional quality when producing "in-house" films
- Films can be rather bulky to carry from one location to another
- A 16mm projector must always be available if the presentation will be given in several locations
- Not as easy to operate as an overhead projector, and more likelihood of a machine breakdown

Videotape

Videotaping (while being popular for quite some time) has become increasingly favored through the accompanying rise of the video-cassette recorder used in the home today. Widely available in a range of formats and cassette size, the medium has now become a valuable resource in business presentations.

Advantages
- Videotape is easily transportable from one location to the next and can be quickly sent to various worldwide areas for immediate viewing (e.g., a business presentation filmed at the home office)
- Very flexible medium (combining visual and auditory experience)
- Tapes can easily be erased, as required
- Can be mailed from one location to another with a minimum of difficulty
- Video can be created "in-house"
- Generally, during audience viewing, room does not have to be entirely dark
- Film available in either monochrome (black and white) or color
- Relatively easy to train an operator to run the equipment

Disadvantages
- Outside video productions can become expensive in relation to "do-it-yourself" filming
- Requires hardware support equipment (camera, monitor and cassette deck)
- Videotapes can quickly become outdated
- Proper videotaping usually requires advanced preparation (such as amount of light required during filming and/or effective recording sound levels)
- Like 16mm film, videotape can easily deteriorate if not properly stored

---

Speaker Tips:

In formal training classes on presentation skills, each talk is usually video-taped, then replayed for individual and group critique. This technique (when done properly) allows for constructive feedback and interchange among the instructor, speaker and participants. Being able to replay a tape and thereby "seeing and hearing" the actual presentation for the second time is probably the best learning experience of all.

In cases where videotaping is not possible, I recommend practicing in front of a large mirror, using an automatic timing device to monitor the planned duration of the talk (these timing mechanisms are now widely available in all electronic and audiovisual stores). Also recommended is the taping of the talk on a standard cassette recorder. Be aware, however, that unless the recorder is of high professional calibre, there will be a distortion (or reduction) in voice quality during playback.

Six Helpful Hints in Front of the Video Camera

Most business presentations are made to a group of peers, in a familiar conference room and under reasonably good conditions. However, as you move up the ladder of success (and, of course, to higher levels of professional speaking), there is always the possibility that you will be requested to deliver a business presentation in front of a "live" video camera. (For example, distributing your video talk on a new product introduction to branch offices around the country.) Here is where the flexibility you have acquired as a professional speaker will aid you greatly.

Your talk will be greatly enhanced if you look and feel your best *just prior to the videotaping* session. Here are a few time-tested guidelines to be aware of before actually going on camera.

1. *Regard food as a high caution area.* To be at your best, eat lightly and sensibly before the presentation, but remember to at least eat *something*. Talking on an empty stomach before a camera will enhance nothing . . . except perhaps hunger pangs. In any case, avoid heavy or fatty-type foods. As a general rule, *never* have anything alcoholic to drink for at least three to four hours before the videotaping. Forget about any notion that it will "relax" you . . . far from it. Actually, it is a depressant and will (among other things), slow down your reflexes and thought processes—something you do not need when being professionally videotaped.

In most cases, food and beverages are not allowed on the set. On sessions that are expected to run over one or two hours, the director will usually provide light snacks off the set. If in doubt, it is always wise to check these details beforehand.

2. *Body conditioning.* Depending upon what level of physical condition you are in, it's important to get a reasonable (but not exhausting) amount of exercise the

day before, since it will generally leave you more physically and mentally relaxed during your talk. For those who *never* exercise, an alternative would be to take a brisk walk for at least one mile on the day before.

Equally important is to get a good night's sleep the day before. If at all possible, try to stay in bed at least one hour longer. Don't worry if you are awake during that last hour; merely keep your eyes closed and relax your body as much as possible.

3. *Rehearsals.* It is very important to go through at least one dress rehearsal with your staff, even if the set is not yet available (or the director is not quite ready for you). In any case, remember to avoid the hot, glaring stage lights until the director is ready to place you on the set. Avoid the temptation to drink large amounts of liquid at this point. You will have plenty of opportunity when "the shoot" has been completed.

4. *Relaxation exercise.* For most speakers, tension has been building to this point, with the adrenalin flowing at a fast rate. This is quite normal and can be counteracted by the deep-breathing exercise taught in this course. While you may be quite anxious now, chances are that these unsettling feelings will quickly leave you within the first few minutes on camera.

5. *Special situations.* If you are being professionally videotaped, and have a special situation that concerns you (such as baldness or a skin problem), it's prudent to contact the producer or director *in advance*. Many of these situations (which can be quite unsettling in your mind) can easily be rectified by makeup, special lighting, dress and positioning before the camera.

6. *Dress.* While dress is always of particular significance in front of a *live* audience, it becomes even more so on videotape. Here are a few basic guidelines for both sexes.

Men: The cardinal rule here is to *avoid complacency*. What seems fine for everyday office wear, may turn out to be a "disaster" on camera. Here are some suggestions:

- Avoid light colored clothing (including white shirts)
- Where possible, select a medium-dark solid color blue, gray or brown (wearing a vest is ideal, since it will give you a more slimming appearance). It comes as a shock to most people when learning that the camera usually *adds 10 to 15 pounds* to the appearance given to the audience!
- Preference should be given to a blue shirt and a *conservative* tie.
- If being taped in the late afternoon or evening, bring your razor, along with a fresh shirt and tie.

Women: With the rapid change in women's fashions for business dress, it's difficult to speculate as to what specific type of clothing to wear. Gone are the days when one could state that women should avoid the "frilly look" or having too much make-up on. That type of advice is not only meaningless, but insulting. As a result (with the exception of bringing a razor to shave for a late taping!), dress rules for women today are approximately the same as described for the men.

As with men, women should avoid light colored clothing, and anything that would convey the impression of a very casual look. Ideally, a medium-dark solid color dress should be worn, with an alternate being a tailored suit with a medium-colored blouse for contrast. Naturally, very shiny jewelry should not be worn in front of the camera, and shoes with very high heels should be avoided.

Audio Recordings

For many years, one of the most dependable and trouble-free of all the audio aids available have been audio recordings. Whether used in a reel-to-reel format (similar to a 16mm reel used in a home projector), or a cassette format (such as the popular size used in most cassette players today), straight audio recordings have remained a popular choice with speakers who require limited audio support on a generally tight budget.

Advantages

- Usually trouble-free operation
- Generally easy to operate with a wide range of record/playback equipment
- Easily transported (or shipped) to different locations
- Relatively small and free of bulk
- Can be produced "in-house" or purchased commercially
- Used properly, provides effective supplement to a wide variety of business presentations

Disadvantages

- Generally requires some form of reinforcement from the presenter
- Since no visual experience is present (except when used in a combined sound/slide show), the recording can easily reflect a lack of professionalism
- Must always be carefully positioned to avoid generating audience boredom

How to Put Audiovisual Aids to Work in Your Presentation

Each of the audiovisual aids described in this chapter carries its own cluster of benefits and possible disadvantages for any given business presentation. The really professional speaker is one who carefully selects the right medium *to best support the message being conveyed*, and *not* because one particular medium is most popular at the moment.

What may work quite well during a presentation in one conference room, may prove to be completely unsatisfactory in a large auditorium. It's therefore very important to always be highly *flexible* when selecting any audiovisual aid . . . to enhance a forthcoming presentation . . . and combining them where necessary to add to the talk even further.

Speaker Tips:

As a general rule, some type of audiovisual support should be used during every business presentation.

As a closing example, let's take the case where a home office team of senior-level managers are visiting the six regional company distribution centers to deliver a business presentation on the *New Accident Reduction Policy* just established by the organization's executive committee.

With the following example, you will specifically see how each audiovisual aid was selected to assist in a particular part of the presentation and further, how these aids can be combined to provide a well-balanced array of support for the talk.

The scenario (using the "mix and match") audiovisual technique might go something like this . . .

Opening Remark: Done by senior team leader

Introduction: Vice president, Personnel (also responsible for plant safety)

Video Message: By the company President (reinforcing importance of topic . . . company expectations, timetables, etc.)

Overhead Transparencies: Two overheads showing overall details of program (done by one member of the presenting team)

Slide Presentation: Ten 35mm slides presented by the assistant team leader which reviews all program details

Flipcharts: Use of two flipcharts to show specific examples both at close of presentation and subsequent question and answer period

Lastly (and as a continuing cardinal rule for every speaker), the process of *pretalk planning* for the right audiovisual support, will always remain a crucial element in the eventual success (or failure) in a forthcoming business presentation.

How to Use the Audiovisual Checklist

The *Audiovisual Support Checklist*, provides a convenient reminder of the various types of equipment which may be required during your business presentation. A filled-in sample is shown in Figure 10-1. Used in conjunction with the Pretalk Room Checklist, it provides a time-tested approach to having the proper support equipment at your presentation every time. It also gives one the opportunity to *combine* both of these forms into just one specifically tailored to your own requirements.

Here's a brief description of each:

Standing Floor Microphone

Most commonly employed when no podium to which a microphone can be attached is used

Lavalier Microphone

A "clip-on" microphone attached to the presenter's clothing (lapel, etc.)

Built-in Public Address System

Where voice amplification is provided throughout the room

Flipchart

Writing pads affixed to a free-standing unit

Blackboard

Slate writing tablet generally in a wooden frame, on rollers

Standing Floor Podium

A unit especially constructed to hold the speaker's papers at a comfortable level/position. Can also contain a light and/or a microphone

Table Podium

Same as above, except made to be placed on a table (instead of the floor)

35 mm Slide Projector

Audiovisual device to project 35 millimeter slides, generally in a circular tray

16 mm Projector

Audiovisual device to project 16 millimeter film generally in a reel-to-reel format

8 mm Projector

Same as 16 mm, except film size is smaller

Cassette Recorder/Playback

Audiovisual device to both record and playback an audio cassette. Very popular for home use

Video Camera

Camera especially designed to record images via videotape

Video Record/Playback Deck

Used in conjunction with video camera to record, then playback processed film through a monitor

AUDIOVISUAL SUPPORT CHECKLIST

Location of Presentation: _4th Floor Conference Room_   Today's Date: _1/20/88_
Date of Presentation: _January 29, 1988_   Room Size: _60' x 125' (App)_
Acoustic Level (Excellent, Average, Poor): _Average_
Room Lighting: (a) Can Be Easily Controlled: _Yes_   (Yes) (No)
    (b) Go From Light To Dark Quickly: _Yes_   (Yes) (No)
    (c) Controlled By Speaker: _Yes_   (Yes) (No)
ALL LIGHTING CONTROLS ON SPEAKER PLATFORM

Item	Usage			Availability		
	Yes	No	Uncertain	Have	Need to Rent	Comments
Standing Floor Microphone		✔				
Lavalier Microphone	✔			✔		HAVE IN-HOUSE
Built-In Public Address System	✔			✔		IN-HOUSE
Flipchart(s) (2 required)	✔			✔		IN-HOUSE
Blackboard(s)		✔		✔		
Standing Floor Podium		✔		✔		
Table Podium		✔		✔		
35mm Slide Projector	✔			✔ (SEE JOHN)		(HE WILL HANDLE)
16mm Projector		✔				
8mm Projector		✔				
Cassette Recorder/Playback		✔				
Video Camera		✔				
Video Record/Playback Deck		✔				
Video Monitor		✔				
Overhead Projector	✔			✔		IN
Pointer (For Speaker)	✔			✔		OUR
Extension Cords	✔			✔		INVENTORY
Spare Equipment Bulbs	✔			✔		

FIGURE 10-1:
Audiovisual Support Checklist (Filled-in Sample of Form 6)

Video Monitor

Audiovisual device (similar to a television screen) which takes video output of playback deck and displays it.

Overhead Projector

Basic device for displaying transparencies on a screen

Pointer

Generally made of wood or aluminum, allowing speaker to point to screen, etc.

Extension Cords

Extra cords in case an electrical extension is needed, between the audiovisual unit and the wall outlet

Spare Equipment Bulbs

Be sure to include extra bulbs to be used in each projector, ''just in case''

Chapter Summary

You have now completed Chapter 10, which illustrated the technique of using audiovisual aids to enhance your next business presentation. This included an in-depth look at the various multi-media support aids available, together with an audiovisual checklist to insure effective preplanning for your next talk,

This puts you in a position to start the next chapter on the art of handling disruptions. Most like to think that audience interruptions (in their many forms) could *never* happen in one of our presentations, but rest assured that sooner or later, it will happen to you.

To be fully prepared for this eventuality, read on.

Memory Joggers

☑ Regardless of the business topic or location given, some form of audiovisual support should be used.

☑ Slides can be mounted either on cardboard or be glass enclosed.

☑ Two of the many advantages of slides are that they can easily be converted to videotape and they can be coupled with audio.

☑ Slide overload can result from attempting to cram too much information onto one slide.

☑ There are two versions of software generally available to a speaker planning to use the overhead projector:

a) Prepared version

b) "Do-It-Yourself" type

☑ Even professionally produced videotape and 16mm film are still subject to deterioration.

☑ Videotape is available in either monochrome or color.

☑ Where appropriate, it is usually desirable to combine several types of audiovisual support during one presentation.

CHAPTER 11

The Art of Handling Disruptions

Occasionally, during a business presentation (and even under the best of circumstances), a disruption will occur. Whether intentional or not, disruptions are a common problem in most presentations.

Naturally, there is always a direct ratio between the *importance* of the speaker to the audience and the degree of interruption, including nonverbal clues such as boredom, or "tuning out" that will be initiated by the group. Whatever the extent of interruption involved, it can prove to be a trying time for the presenter.

For most speakers, usually one or two minor interruptions can be reasonably overlooked (conversely, the same would hold true for the participants). If ignored however, the seemingly minor disruption can grow into a major disrupting factor—and definitely reduce the effectiveness of the presentation itself. Put a bit differently, by simply ignoring a disruption for any length of time, chances are that it will *not* automatically correct itself. Worse yet, by delaying a counter reaction to end the disruption, the problem (once recognized) may already be out of control. To complicate the scenario further, one of the principles of group psychology begins to take hold, causing the disruptive behavior of one (or several participants) to become "contagious" to others in the audience. If this type of situation is allowed to develop, the presentation becomes in real danger of turning into a fiasco. While this is rarely a "black or white" type situation, it usually ends up with the audience becoming quite unsettled, or even worse, submerged in general apathy.

Three Guidelines for Handling Disruptions

Before proceeding into the various types of potential problem participants, let's highlight *three fundamental guidelines that must be kept in mind at all times.*

Guideline 1: Always Handle the Problem Early. As with all potential disturbances, it is far easier to identify and correct a problem in its early stages, rather than ignoring it and having to confront it when it has become more serious. Put another way, handle it early on . . . before it starts to handle you!

Guideline 2: Never Embarrass or Put a Troublemaker Down in Front of a Group. Let's face it . . . while this may afford you immediate satisfaction *at that moment in time*, it is almost a certainty that you will lose out in the long run. Certainly, your annoyance may be fully justified, but in expressing same, you will probably trigger another principle of group psychology which creates sympathy and empathy for the "underdog" (in this case, the participant whom you have just lashed out at). More than likely, the audience will begin to resent you for the embarrassment of the individual you have just "put down." The end result can be a wave of demotivation being experienced by the majority of those listening to you. Obviously, this is a situation to avoid at all times!

Speaker Tips:

In handling any type of disruption, never lose your composure (verbally and/or non-verbally) in front of the audience, no matter how justified you may have been.

Six Clues on Recognizing a Problem Early and Offsetting It

1. As a general rule, the earlier you establish a close rapport with the audience, the least likelihood there will be of *any* problem developing with an individual.

2. A potential problem can be created with people arriving late (from a few moments to several minutes after the talk has begun). In most cases, it's merely a few seconds of distraction (especially for the speaker). Best advice is to ignore the distraction completely and continue speaking in the same measured tone.

3. Be especially aware of the room environment both *prior to* and during your talk. By environment, I mean heating, air conditioning, lighting, outside noise and the like, that can distract the audience through no fault of their own. For example, if the room is much too warm (with a corresponding lack of ventilation) some early danger signs are "drooping" eyelids, people starting to lose interest, and beginning to doze off. Immediate action is called for! Either, (a) stop the

---

Speaker Tips (continued):

talk momentarily and remedy the condition yourself, (b) request the building superintendent to correct the condition, or if all else fails (c) call for a two-minute "stretch-break" and continue using short breaks as required.

4. Watch for interruptions caused by someone entering the room with an urgent message (usually a telephone call). In any group over 10 people, if this happens once, rest assured that others in your audience will likely be called out. The best advise here is to *not let it happen at all* by requesting a "no-disturbances" sign on the door, and informing the audience early in your opening of this request. As with many of the other problems listed here, it's wise to ignore the "urgent call" situation as best you can. But ... *never* show annoyance, since the person being called out of the room is not at fault.

5. Take a constant reading of the non-verbal clues being exhibited by the participants. Things like a furrowed brow, a hand hesitantly going up in the air then being lowered again, two people staring at your last slide and whispering to each other could mean you have begun to "lose the audience". Better take a quick reality check and ask a few open-ended questions of the group to let them "come-alive" again.

6. If your talk will run over one hour, will conclude after the normal lunch hour has begun, or will go well past the time that most people would normally leave, make certain that those individuals who must leave early are seated in the *rear* of the room. If this is not possible (and the group is fairly small), announce in advance that "so and so" has to leave early, and state that you appreciate that he/she is attending. If you haven't done this, and you see people starting to leave, stop the presentation for a moment and ask for a show of hands of those who have to leave early. It's only common courtesy, and it will make everyone feel more relaxed.

Guideline 3: Never Lose Your Temper During the Presentation. Regardless of the topic, room environment and degree of complexity involved, the audience expects the presenter to be the true authority figure in the room, to use that power wisely during the presentation, and to convey the presentation message in a courteous adult manner.

Accordingly, and regardless of how one may become provoked, the cardinal rule in effective public speaking is to *never* lose control over one's emotions during a business presentation. Granted, in certain cases (such as where one is deliberately provoked . . . for whatever reason) this maintenance of control may seem like an impossible task; but rest assured that it isn't. The main point here is that the *instant* the audience *perceives* you have lost control, the presentation becomes a candidate for instant failure. *Never* . . . never let this happen to you.

Speaker Tips:

If you do lose your temper inadvertently, all is not lost. You can still come out a winner by following these simple rules:

A) Take a deep breath, relax as best you can, and apologize to the person at whom your anger was directed. (At this point, you will immediately win over three-quarters of the audience who were becoming angry with you as a result of this behavior.)

B) As an act of common courtesy, explain why the situation upset you, but immediately follow the explanation with a "closure-type" second apology (now you have probably won over the remainder in the audience who were upset with your reaction).

C) Immediately swing back into your talk as if nothing had happened. Continue the presentation in the same measured pace as before. However, if at all possible, avoid the use of humor for the balance of the talk. Remember, you are still "on probation" (so to speak) in the audience's eyes.

Let's now turn our attention to the types of people who cause disruptions and—most importantly—how to cope with them effectively.

Characteristics of Problem Participants and Strategies for Dealing With Them

There are six broad but very realistic categories of individuals that can cause real problems for the speaker. Let's review them one at a time, outlining the characteristics involved, together with a recommended counterstrategy.

Type 1: The Chatterbox

Overt Characteristics. In the order of participant problem types, these individuals are probably the most disruptive of all, since (for whatever reason) they never seem to stop talking from the moment they enter the room until the presentation has been concluded!

People who fall within this category appear to take a great deal of self-satisfaction in carrying on both *direct* (face-to-face) and *indirect* (looking at the speaker, but whispering discreetly to their neighbor) conversation that (unfortunately) begins to disrupt the flow of information which the speaker is attempting to convey at that moment. In certain situations, they will even attempt to carry on a conversation with another member of the audience (either across the table or room), completely ignoring what is being presented. Any way viewed, this poses a serious threat to the speaker, and one which has to be squelched as quickly as possible.

Speaker Counterstrategy. The most efficient method to terminate this annoyance is to draw the constant talker back into the mainstream of the presentation without making it too obvious . . . yet at the same time, *as quickly as possible.*

This task, while appearing rather simple, is actually quite complex; while it must be accomplished rapidly, the presenter cannot make it too obvious, and therefore, run the risk of appearing too "heavy-handed" in front of the audience. The strategy therefore, calls for the speaker to periodically solicit the opinion of the individual(s) about what has just been presented. Obviously, the "chatterbox" will not be able to offer an opinion, since no listening was taking place at all! The strategy then, is for the speaker to quickly move on (avoiding any further embarrassment to the "chatterbox"), but within a few moments, *again solicit the opinion about what has just been said.* (Naturally, in the interim, and not to make it too obvious, the presenter should also call on a few other people.)

Use of this strategy over several minutes will generally discourage the "chatterbox" from further interruptions. A nice side benefit involved here, is that this strategy will also discourage any additional side conversations with people who were located near the constant talker . . . and who might be tempted to initiate the process themselves.

All in all, a subtle, yet very effective technique can be used by the speaker to stop the disruption, but as with all of the techniques described here, must be used with extreme caution.

For each of the problem situations described, two examples of the counterstrategy will be offered. The first two are given below.

Example One

"I find your comment very controversial, Tom . . . and have the feeling that many people in this room will have strong opinions either way. Let's see if I'm right on this. How do you feel about this, Jack?"

Example Two

"Well, I see my last comment appears to have caused some concern among you. I'm curious as to how many in the audience agree with my point of view. Let's start with you, Jack . . . agree or disagree?"

Type 2: The Overly Dependent Person

Speaker Tips:

An alternate strategy to stop the chatterbox is to *gaze* at him/her while talking. If that doesn't work, the ultimate fallback position would be to stop talking and *stare* at the person until they stop talking. It's a bit tricky for the speaker, but usually a very effective technique.

Overt Characteristics. In direct contrast to the constant talker, this type of participant will *never* cause a verbal disturbance, but nevertheless becomes a problem participant for the speaker by acting in the exact reverse manner. As a result, this type of problem participant cannot be ignored by the speaker . . . and must be dealt with accordingly.

The "I need your help" types can easily be identified by their overt hesitancy, lack of self-confidence and heavy dependency upon others. Accordingly, when attending a business presentation, it is extremely important to them not to look foolish *in any way* in front of their peers; hence, they will usually *not participate in any manner*.

This unfortunate situation is triggered by constant levels of insecure feeling, leading to the fear of expressing an independent opinion, even though they might feel quite strongly about a point being raised (and inwardly, would really like to state their opinions). Accordingly, left alone during a presentation, they will usually *not* participate, and at the very best (if forced to), will always become part of the majority opinion, never oppose a group consensus, and *never* verbally disagree with another participant (or the speaker) even during the liveliest of question and answer periods.

Speaker Counterstrategy. Although heavily dependent upon others, this group of individuals usually do have some very productive and creative ideas. The strategy therefore, must be built around drawing these thoughts out in a constructive, *non-threatening* manner . . . building self-confidence and gently paving the way for a higher level of involvement.

The technique involved is a series of *non-threatening* probes (or questions) asked by the speaker to this person and several others around the room. In other words, a question raised wherein the answer is somewhat obvious, always correct, yet not demeaning. Done properly, the "I need your help" participant will easily respond to the first question (which of course, has been carefully prepared to build up his or her confidence level). A few moments later in the presentation, a second question is asked—of perhaps a slightly different nature—but still non-threatening. Once this is accomplished, the speaker is well on the way to making this participant a truly productive member of the audience.

In passing, the presenter should never forget that when dealing with this type, *extreme caution* must be taken during probing to avoid having the individual feel threatened in any way. In any case, it's always a *delicate* task involved, and one which should never be treated casually by the speaker.

Example One

"Well, looks like the Management Committee has finally agreed completely on the recommendations just established by the Policy Committee. I know that this is a good course of action for us to follow, but before we make it official, I wanted to make absolutely sure that everyone here is for it. I think there are just two or three that we haven't heard from yet. Mmmmm. . . . How about you Fran? Do you agree with the others?"

Example Two

"Guess we have a true consensus here. Out of the fifteen present in the room, looks like at least twelve of you think affirmatively on the proposed recommendation. But, before closing the meeting, just wanted to make sure that we have heard from everyone on this. Let's see, I need to hear from both George and Fran on this. Can we start with you, Fran?"

Speaker Tips:

If the overly dependent person still is too shy or insecure to answer, quickly ask the same question of another person. However, to spare further embarrassment, try not to ask the person sitting next to that individual ... but direct your question to someone as far away as possible.

Type 3: The Superiority Syndrome

Overt Characteristics. Whatever the type or level of business presentation being given, this type of individual will focus their main energy and attention level to challenging the presenter both overtly and subtly.

During various parts of the presentation, these individuals will either contradict the speaker, or (at best) introduce a "clarifying remark" to others in the audience. While this rather sinister type of psychological game can be played at all levels of management, it is most effective when the "I know better than you. . ." type is of a higher rank than the speaker. In many cases, in order to strengthen their position of "dominance and superiority", they will maneuver themselves into position to give a final overview to the group, of what has just been presented . . . then adding their own specific opinions, which usually are slightly different from the points that the speaker was attempting to make! Cunningly done, this overview (or summary) will appear to the rest of the audience as almost an "afterthought," but one (of course), made with high significance.

Speaker Counterstrategy. Here's a perfect example where "The best defense is a good offense!"

As a starter, the presenter must be aware of the fact that these people strongly seek (and need) recognition to fuel their egos, especially if they are in a critical stage of building their own power base. While this could be perceived as a disguise to compensate for their own feelings of insecurity, it is important to supply them with the required recognition, but *controlled by the speaker, not* the participant. The counterstrategy here is in two parts.

1. As a starter make certain to call upon them *early* during the presentation *before* they have had an opportunity to pick the "perfect moment" to oppose you.
2. Secondly, immediately after offering their opinion, discreetly announce that while a good point was made, there may be several differing opinions on the subject, and quickly ask the others in the audience for their comments.

While there are never any guarantees, in most cases, this type of pro-active counterstrategy effectively discourages the "I know better than you. . ." types, or at the very least, reduces their disruptive tactics to a minimum.

Example One

"Well John, that was certainly an interesting point that you made. In my opinion, it brings up several related issues, both pro and con. How about you Susan . . . What are your thoughts on this?"

Example Two

"Thanks for your views, John. In fact, I'm sure that several others in the room can add even additional value to the subject. Randy . . . I know that you generally prefer a more conservative approach to this type of subject. Really would like to hear your thoughts on this."

Speaker Tips:

- Don't be discouraged if this technique does not work each time. Remember that you are probably dealing with a "power authority" which is probably the most difficult to handle.
- An ultimate fallback position here would be to draw the person aside *after* the presentation, tactfully explaining the situation and requesting their help in terminating same. However, in doing so, always stress the fact that you are *sure* they are doing it *inadvertently.* Remember that their ego's are involved!

Type 4: The Very Important Person

Overt Characteristics. Regardless of the time the presentation has been scheduled to start, it is practically guaranteed that this type will arrive *after* the meeting has begun. At the very best, they will be barely on time, and usually the last ones to enter the room.

Generally, the V.I.P.'s entrance centers around a frenzied, harried state, usually making certain (both verbally and non-verbally) to show others in the audience the "sacrifice" being made by merely having this person attend! Once seated, this type will usually convey a mild sense of annoyance when catching the speaker's attention . . . to make certain that the message is also clear to the speaker.

Many additional variations are also possible on occasion. This same person will either be called out of the presentation for an "urgent" phone call or else, spend the majority of time furiously writing notes to himself for apparent follow-up. Immediately after the conclusion of the presentation, a favorite tactic of this type is (while they are rushing out of the door), to loudly call out to several others in the audience to call him (or her) as soon as possible. Clearly, a distraction in every sense of the word!

Speaker Counterstrategy. The "I'm too busy, but I came anyway . . ." type has to be handled with extreme care, since these people seek constant ego reinforcement to fuel their sense of self-esteem. Anything that is perceived to be a threat to that, is dealt with in a very negative sense (i.e., this type when threatened, has been known to walk out of a meeting "in disgust" since "Nothing worthwhile is being said . . .").

The counterstrategy is simple and direct. It is that immediately upon their arrival (even though it might be late), *involve* them in some type of task where specific follow-up is required. Obviously, the task will always be perceived as a high importance area.

Example One

"Hi Sam, really glad that you could join us. We've saved a chair for you right in the middle. We are about to discuss the morale situation in the Accounting Department, and I know you are an expert in this area. Would greatly appreciate it if you could stay a few minutes after the presentation to make certain that we have covered all of the follow-up items required."

Example Two

"Thank you all for coming today. The matter of poor morale within our Accounting Department is a serious one. That's why I'm glad Sam could join us today. Since he is so knowledgeable in this area, I'm going to ask him to keep careful notes during my presentation and help us with the required follow-up during the next few days. So . . . thanks for joining us Sam. It's a pleasure to have you here."

```
┌─────────────────────────────────────────────────────────────┐
│  Speaker Tips:                                                │
│                                                               │
│    • The alternate strategy here is basically the same as     │
│      described in type 3; the superiority syndrome. The only  │
│      difference is that the "V.I.P." probably has an even more │
│      inflated ego, so, an even higher level of tact is        │
│      required.                                                │
│    • But ... in both types, never be hesitant in drawing them │
│      aside after the meeting, explaining the situation and    │
│      requesting their help.                                   │
└─────────────────────────────────────────────────────────────┘
```

Type 5: The Chronic Complainer

Overt Characteristics. While perhaps not as sinister as some of the types already discussed, this type appears to take particular delight in pointing out all of the details that are either unacceptable, or are detracting from the meeting.

Complaints are usually numerous and quite specific. They can range anywhere from the room being stuffy, hot or cold, to the coffee break arriving late, having the coffee "not taste right", sitting in an uncomfortable chair . . . and so on (I'm sure any experienced speaker could add at least ten additional complaint items!) Interestingly enough, whether the displeasure is expressed verbally or nonverbally, this type appears to take a subtle pleasure in expressing dissatisfaction with just about every aspect of the meeting.

Speaker Counterstrategy. The most effective rule to follow is one of taking the initiative *before* this type has a chance to voice the complaint. Put another way, staying very alert for any type of negative situation—but once discovered, picking up and handling it in the most efficient manner possible. (Granted, on occasion, easier said than done.)

By handling each situation in this manner, the speaker will at least begin to discourage the complainer from continuing to disrupt the talk. However, as with all of the problems discussed so far, a heavy degree of patience, tact and diplomacy is called for on the part of the presenter.

Example One

"Before we begin the presentation, I'd like to point out that I've contacted our maintenance department about the defective air conditioning, and they promised to have it fixed within the next few minutes. Sorry about that folks . . . if it's not corrected by the coffee break, I'll personally check on it again."

Example Two

"I agree with you Nancy . . . the room is a bit overcrowded. Normally, we do not have twenty participants during this type of presentation. However, due to the overwhelming demand, we decided to increase the class size today. To offset the space problem, I'm planning to take both longer and more frequent coffee/coke breaks throughout the day. And . . . with a bit of luck, even end the presentation by 4:00 PM instead of 5:00!"

Speaker Tips:

Always keep in mind that it's easiest to lose your temper with the chronic complainer. Conversely, the watchword is patience, blended with a bit more patience. But never, single this person out as the "only one who is complaining" for the audience will surely turn against you.

Type 6: The Authority Figure

Overt Characteristics. Although similar in many respects to the "I know better than you" type, this group concentrates their efforts on letting everyone in the audience know how important they are to the organization.

Naturally, this type of individual is of a higher rank than most, and highlights the fact that he is responsible for the group and should be accorded a *special* status. While on occasion, they may challenge the speaker (if that suits their purpose at the time). Their main objective in attending the presentation is to reinforce the fact that they are in a position of authority. Hence by their mere presence, they lend *credibility* to the meeting.

Generally then, each response they make during a presentation is usually made in such a way as to convey the "final word" on the issue—in either an obvious or quite subtle manner. Obviously, this can prove to be an *extremely delicate situation* for the presenter, since no honest conveying of information can be transmitted to an audience when even the slightest hint of intimidation is present. Worse yet, the "I'm really in charge here" type can be your own boss!

Speaker Counterstrategy. Done of course with great care at all times! The strategy to be employed is to first acknowledge the respect due to this individual (since this person has reached a high position of authority, and is entitled to this business courtesy).

Secondly, immediately following this acknowledgement of status, there should be a carefully worded question that will encourage this individual to share some of his or her experiences based upon this achieved status. Put another way, this counterstrategy involves turning elevated rank (which could be a formidable psychological barrier to the meeting) into a real plus, based upon the person's prior experience and background within the presentation being delivered.

Normally, people who have obtained this type of high rank will not usually be at meetings (as part of an audience) with personnel of much lower status. However, as experience has taught us, this type of situation will happen from time to time, and the presenter should always be ready to deal with it.

Example One

"Well, looks like we can't seem to reach a consensus on the proper timing for the new budget cycle. Nick, we could use the benefit of your experience in matters like this. May I ask . . . What should our next steps be?"

CHECKLIST FOR HANDLING DISRUPTIONS

Date of Planned Talk: _____

Type	Individual's Name	Countermeasures to be Employed
Chatterbox	Dorothy Favarese	• Ask her opinion about Company Sales projection • Request her advice on training department support
Overly Dependent	Nancy Raymond	• Ask her if she agrees with group on new sales brochure • Follow up with her opinion on choice of color for front cover (everyone likes blue)
Superiority		
V.I.P.	Linda Shield	• Request her critique of the new audiovisual sales aids • Ask her to help you with required follow-up after meeting concludes
Chronic Complainer		
Authority Figure	Nick Brown (VP, sales)	• Early on, thank Nick for taking time to join meeting • Ask him to share viewpoints on next year's sales forecast

FIGURE 11-1:
Checklist For Handling Disruptions (Filled-in Sample of Form 7)

Example Two

"I realize that our new compensation plan is a radical departure from the one we've had during the past five years . . . and for some of you this could prove to be an unsettling time. Let me assure you however, that senior management spent a great deal of time in developing this, and considers it to be far superior in every respect.

"Nick . . . I know that you served on the task force for this, and I was wondering whether you would mind sharing some of your thoughts with us. It would certainly be reassuring to hear from one of the senior executives who was one of the prime architects of the new plan itself!"

Note: With this approach, the speaker has covered most contingencies. For example, even if Nick declined to comment, the speaker would have won the respect of the audience by affording Nick the respect due his position . . . and extending a normal business courtesy.

Speaker Tips:

Always keep in mind that the authority figure has *the authority*! Of all the six types presented, use the greatest care with this one. Never employ the recommended counterstrategy unless you are on reasonably safe ground.

As with all of these problem types, pretalk preparation will go a long way in helping to defuse the potential roadblock before it is encountered. Figure 11-1, checklist for handling disruptions, shows how the form could be used in a typical business presentation where the speaker was reasonably familiar with the audience.

Chapter Summary

You have now finished Chapter 11 which described the art of handling disruptions. You learned the basic guidelines involved, together with characteristics of six types of problem participants and the specific strategies for dealing with them.

This puts you in line for the reading of Chapter 12, the final one in the workbook, which deals directly with the "coach approach" and the four steps which practically guarantee your entry into the world of more professional business presentations.

Memory Joggers

☑ If ignored, a seemingly minor disruption can grow into a major factor.

☑ There are three fundamental guidelines to keep in mind when handling problem participants:

- Always handle the problem early.
- Never embarrass or put a troublemaker down in front of a group.
- Never lose your temper.

☑ An efficient counterstrategy for the "Constant Talker" is to draw him or her back into the mainstream of the presentation as quickly as possible.

CHAPTER 12

The Coach Approach: Four Steps to a Better Presentation

In order to become more proficient in business presentations, you must first discover what current deficiencies you may have acquired over the years. While this may seem like a simple thing to accomplish, rest assured that, in most cases, it is *not*. The fact is, no one likes to be judged, especially in areas where ego or self-esteem is involved. But by learning your weak points, you will have a key starting point to put you on the road toward becoming a more effective speaker—whether it be a talk on the monthly review of absenteeism for a group of first-line supervisors, or a formal presentation of year-end operating results to the executive committee.

Once you can establish those specific areas requiring improvement, a checklist for personal improvement can be implemented, giving you a concrete basis for measuring your new skill level.

There are two ways to go about this. The first (if it is available to you) is to actually have a business associate in the audience who would critique your next presentation during the normal course of a working day. If this is not possible, the second option is to do it at home using your spouse, close friend, or relative as a "coach."

Regardless of the option selected, try to get this done as quickly as possible. In doing so, you will be removing one of the most common barriers to success—those unfavorable speaking traits that you now have, but will soon discard.

Let's look at the four steps to a more proficient business presentation and how they work.

Step 1: Select a Topic For Your Practice Talk

The first step is to select a topic for your talk that will be critiqued. For those of you who elect to work with a coach at home, but find it difficult to choose a topic, here are fifteen suggestions which can help you get started.

Suggested Topics
- Why I Prefer City Living
- There's No Place Like Suburbia
- The Trouble with Kids Today
- The Secrets of a Successful Marriage
- Learning to Love Your In-laws
- The Best Vacation Spot in the World
- Why I Love Rainy Days
- How to Keep a Man (or Woman) Really Happy
- Birthdays Should Be Banned
- Strategies in Selecting a Good Wine
- Being a Workaholic Has Certain Benefits
- How to Retire and Enjoy It
- The Advantages of Working for a Small Company
- When to Talk Back to Your Boss

. . . Or, if you are really daring, how about:
- How to Deliver a Winning Business Presentation!

Decide Where to Give Your Talk

The next thing you need to do is decide on a time and place to deliver your talk. Presenters, over the years, when using this process with managers, the great majority (even though they had the opportunity) did not want to attempt this first critiqued talk in front of peers at the workplace. Instead, they preferred to give the talk in the privacy of their home. A few have even suggested that they accomplish this alone, speaking in front of a mirror. In a word, *don't*! One can never hope to play the parts of speaker and coach at the same time. It simply does not work, will prove frustrating, and is a waste of your time.

Step 2: Choose a Coach and Review the Critique Procedure

Once you have selected a topic, a time, and a place for your talk, spend a few moments with your chosen coach and review all of the main headings and categories in the *Coach Evaluation Checklist* (Form 8).

There are four main categories given:

1. Presentation Format
2. Personal Dynamics
3. Mannerisms
4. Eyes

A fifth area, "Miscellaneous," is included for any additional comments from your coach that don't fit into the four main categories.

Let's take a closer look at each of the four basic headings.

1. *Presentation Format:* Focuses on the overall structure of the talk, from the opening to the ending, with emphasis on continuity of points made
2. *Personal Dynamics:* Shifts emphasis from the presentation to the individual characteristics exhibited by the speaker—especially highlighting levels of professionalism
3. *Mannerisms:* Those specific traits exhibited by the presenter, with particular emphasis on any movement or gesture of a distracting nature
4. *Eyes:* Special focus on the eye contact and "sweep" (so essential to a really professional business presentation)

How to Complete the Coach Evaluation Checklist

A glance at the checklist shows that the speaker (Jack Barnes) was relying on Fred Kline as his coach. In selecting a person to handle this function, the following guidelines should be observed:

1. The coach should know the speaker reasonably well (in other words, not a "total stranger").
2. Correspondingly, it should also be a person who can be completely impartial and unbiased in his or her evaluation.
3. Avoid having one's manager or subordinate fill the coach function. It's far better to have someone in the same peer group.
4. Ideally (and if at all possible) the coach would be someone who would be able to *reverse* roles with the speaker, and, at a later date, be coached by the other individual.

The first thing you should do is complete the top portion of the form, leaving blank the lines that say "Starting Time" and "Ending Time." These lines and the balance of the form should be filled in by your coach, as unobtrusively as possible, *while the talk is proceeding.*

A word of caution here. While it may be a temptation for the coach to complete all the categories after the talk has concluded, *don't let this happen.* Even under the best of circumstances, important characteristics of your talk can be easily forgotten a few moments later.

COACH EVALUATION CHECKLIST

Speaker: *Jack Barnes*   Coach: *Fred Kline*

Title of Talk: *SECOND QUARTER EARNINGS FORECAST*

Date: *May 11, 1987*   Audience Size: *10 (approx.)*

Location: *Main Conference Room*   Planned Length of Talk *15 minutes*

Type of Audio-Visual Used *Flipchart*   Starting Time *9:30 AM*   Ending Time *9:55 AM*

(RAN 10 MINUTES OVER)

Category	Satisfactory	Needs Improvement
Presentation format Well organized opening	✔ *Got everyone's attention*	
Good continuity	✔ *Reasonably so*	
Clear points made		*Statistics a bit unclear* ⊗
Effective ending		*Seemed to drift a bit at the end* ⊗
Personal dynamics Enthusiastic		*Could be at a higher level* ⊗
Persuasive	✔	
Good presence	✔	
In control	*Except at the ending when you got flustered* ✔	
Mannerisms Nervousness		*At the end, just prior to close* ⊗
Distracting gestures		*Kept rubbing left ear!* ⊗
Voice projection	✔ *Strong*	
Modulation	✔	
Tone	✔ *Good*	
(other) *None*		
Eyes Maintained audience contact	✔ *Reasonably OK*	
Occasional sweep	✔ *Well done*	
(other) *None*		
Miscellaneous		

Concentrate on a stronger ending (and watch your timing)

Watch out for ear rubbing/pulling (very distracting!!)

FIGURE 12-1:
Coach Evaluation Checklist (Filled-in Sample of Form 8)

Note that in each main category the coach should record comments for each line item, as appropriate. The following guidelines are suggested:

1. *Where a category is satisfactory:* Place a check mark (✔) within the appropriate box. If something in the talk is especially well done, write an abbreviated comment.

2. *Where a category needs improvement:* Place an "X" within the selected box. If at all possible, describe *why* that particular portion within the talk was not satisfactory. This will be especially important during the feedback session when you review the talk with your coach.

Why a Coach Is Your Best Review Method

Using a coach—a mentor, business associate, and so forth—is the most effective method of reviewing your talk. Ideally, the coach should be someone who has viewed an actual presentation of yours, and can then give you direct and confidential feedback on a firsthand basis.

Speaker Tips:

It's almost impossible to view yourself in a completely unbiased manner during a talk. That's why choosing an unbiased observer as your coach can prove to be invaluable help in improving your presentation technique.

Step 3: Give Your Talk and Have It Critiqued

At this point you should have

1. Selected a topic for your first talk.
2. Chosen an appropriate location.
3. Arranged for a coach to complete the *Coach Evaluation Checklist*.

Now you're ready to give your initial talk with the coach in the audience. To see how the procedure works, let's return to our filled-in sample of the Coach Evaluation Checklist, and see how our speaker, Jack Barnes did.

At first glance, it appears that Jack's talk went reasonably well. However, Jack's coach, Fred Kline, noted the following areas for improvement:

• The talk ran ten minutes over the allotted time.
• Several statistics were difficult to understand.
• The ending was not as strong as it should have been.
• Enthusiasm was OK, but could have been a bit higher.

How to Prepare Your Coach for the Critique Process

For a coach's feedback to be especially helpful, both positive and negative aspects of the talk should be stressed. However, as in all coaching procedures, the positive aspects of the talk should be stressed first. The following questions cover some of the important areas that a coach should be aware of when critiquing a presentation.

Presentation Format

Was the opening really effective? _____

If not, what specifically can be done to improve the next talk?

_____

Was a good bridging technique used? _____

Was the talk geared to the audience's background/expectation level?

_____

Did the audience appear to have its interest maintained throughout?

If not, what specifically went wrong? _____

_____

Was the closing done smoothly? Specify. _____

_____

Were all audience questions handled properly? Why or why not?

_____

Did the speaker exit gracefully from the stage or podium? _____

_____

Nonverbal Signals (Body Language)

Did you note any signs of anxiety or extreme nervousness? _____

_____

Did the speaker appear to be generally relaxed and in a comfortable posture in front of the audience? ___

How to Prepare Your Coach for the Critique Process (*Continued*)

Were there any distracting mannerisms, such as:

_____	ear pulling	_____ collar tugging
_____	rubbing eyes/nose	_____ hands in pocket
_____	excessive use of "uhmm" or other sound	_____ frequent clearing of throat
_____	"death grip" on podium or other prop	_____ lack of eye contact with audience

Speech Technique

Did the speaker articulate properly? (any word slurring, mumbling? Was each word spoken clearly?) ____

_____

Did the speaker make effective use of the pause? (proper timing, not overdone? _____

_____

Were the pitch and tone appropriate? (effective mood created? right emphasis of words? enough variation?) _____

_____

Was the pacing satisfactory? (too fast? too slow?) _____

Was the speaker's volume level acceptable? (any distortion? heard clearly throughout room?) _____

_____

Audiovisual Support

If audiovisuals were *not* used, did it reduce the effectiveness of the presentation in any way? _____

_____

If so, which audiovisual medium should have been employed, and how would it have helped? _____

_____

General

If applicable:

Was the room lighting adequate?

Air conditioning and/or room ventilation?

Room acoustics . . . use of microphone where necessary

Was pointer required, and (if so) used to best advantage?

Was podium used for maximum effectiveness?

- The speaker was nervous at the end of the talk.
- The ear pulling proved distracting to the audience.

It is assumed in this example that the coach reviewed the checklist with the speaker, via a short critique on those elements of the talk requiring correction, *shortly after the talk had been concluded.*

Speaker Tips:

As with all coaching activities, it is always a good practice to debrief by first mentioning the points that were *done well,* then going into the constructive suggestions for improvement.

After you complete your talk, you will need to make a decision.

1) If both you and the coach believe that the talk was not truly representative of your current speaking skills (for example, if you were extremely nervous because someone was formally critiquing your talk), then a second talk should be attempted as soon as possible. If this is done however, try to speak on a different topic to avoid a biased evaluation.

2) On the other hand, if the consensus is that the checklist items were reasonably valid, you are ready for the next step.

Speaker Tips:

If your talk has been videotaped, both you and your coach can critique the video as soon as possible after the talk has concluded. You can then pay special attention to the areas noted as needing improvement.

If you have the time, you may wish to videotape your practice presentation in a room with just the video operator and coach present. The coach can complete the Coach Evaluation Checklist. When your actual presentation is videotaped, you will have an invaluable "before" and "after" analysis of how well your talk has progressed.

If videotaping is not possible, the cassette player-recorder will also help you, though to a more limited degree. Although there may be some distortion, the timing of the talk can be accurately measured, as well as the use of modulation, pause, and pacing.

WARNING: Always advise a group if your talk is being recorded— even if you have no intention of using the tape for anything other than your own private use.

CHECKLIST FOR PERSONAL IMPROVEMENT

Category	Comments Noted	Personal Reaction
Presentation format Well organized opening		
Good continuity		CHECK INTO THIS: NEVER REALIZED IT WAS HAPPENING
Clear points made ⊗	STATISTICS WERE NOT PRESENTED WELL	
Effective ending ⊗	WEAK ENDING	NEED MORE DYNAMICS HERE
Personal Dynamics Enthusiastic ⊗	COULD USE MORE ENTHUSIASM	THOUGHT IT WAS FINE ? NOT SURE HOW TO CORRECT
Persuasive		
Good presence		
In control ⊗	LOSE CONTROL WHEN I GET FLUSTERED	IMPORTANT POINT: MUST CORRECT THIS
Mannerisms Nervousness ⊗		PROBABLY WHEN I GET FLUSTERED
Distracting gestures	NERVOUS PRIOR TO CLOSE RUBBING AND PULLING OF LEFT EAR	THIS HAS GOT TO BE CORRECTED ASAP!
Voice projection		
Modulation		
Tone		
(other)		
Eyes Maintained audience contact		
Occasional sweep		
(other)		
Miscellaneous		

FIGURE 12-2:
Checklist for Personal Improvement (Filled-in Sample of Form 9)

Step 4: Complete the Checklist for Personal Improvement

To provide you with a specific list of speaking traits that require improvement, you need only to review the areas marked for corrective action on the *Coach Evaluation Checklist* (Form 8), and then transfer them onto your filled-in *Checklist for Personal Improvement* (Form 9).

To get a better idea of how to complete Form 9, let's return to our earlier example of Jack Barnes, speaker, and his coach, Fred Kline. Based on Fred's remarks (See Figure 12-1), Jack was able to complete Form 9. His filled-in sample is shown on page 00.

In the first column, Jack quickly paraphrased the *Needs Improvement* section from the evaluation checklist onto the *Comments Noted*. After reviewing this (together with a few helpful comments from his coach, Jack was able to identify elements for his specific action plan via the *Personal Reaction* column.

An important point to bear in mind here is that the Checklist for Personal Improvement should never be considered as an *all-inclusive* list showing where correction is required. It is merely an important *starting point* displaying general areas that have been initially earmarked for correction.

How to Analyze Audience Reaction

Whether the presentation lasts for just a few minutes, or is over an hour in length, the perceptive speaker can continuously monitor the audience reaction to the presentation, and when necessary, take quick remedial action steps to correct the situation.

This analysis of audience reaction takes in both verbal and non-verbal clues. For example, here are several examples from each category and how the talk can be modified accordingly.

Let's take a closer look at Figure 12-3 (For this illustration only, the checklist contains *tips* on "symptoms" and "how to handle." In actual use, the speaker would have completed both sides of the form).

Note that the form has been segregated by both verbal and non-verbal audience clues. Further, the left-hand side of the checklist has space for those symptoms arising from the audience which could cause potential problems; while the right-hand side encourages the speaker to list the remedial action that was taken (or should have been employed) to improve the effectiveness of the talk.

If possible, this audience reaction strategy checklist should be completed as quickly as possible after the presentation has been concluded. While this can be done independently by the speaker, it would be further enhanced with input from the coach.

The purpose of this checklist is both simple and very effective. It has been created to specifically pinpoint what type of problems have arisen during the talk, and correspondingly, how they were handled. Done over the period of several

AUDIENCE REACTION STRATEGY CHECKLIST	
Verbal Clues	
Symptoms	Remedial Action Plan
1. QUESTIONS CALLED FOR, BUT NONE FORTHCOMING ... EXCEPT OCCASIONAL "CROSS TALK" AMONG PARTICIPANTS AND OTHER VERBAL BOREDOM SIGNS (IN THE NON-INTENTIONAL CATEGORY)	1A. BEGIN SELECTIVELY PROBING MEMBERS OF THE AUDIENCE, SOLICITING THEIR OPINION 1B. DELIBERATELY ASK A PROVOCATIVE QUESTION FROM THE GROUP — ONE YOU KNOW, ABOUT WHICH STRONG OPINIONS (BOTH PRO AND CON) ALREADY EXIST 1C. ASK A QUESTION, THEN INFORM THE AUDIENCE THAT YOU WILL GIVE YOUR OWN OPINION FIRST, THEN SEE HOW MANY AGREE OR DISAGREE WITH YOU
2. DISRUPTIONS FROM PARTICIPANTS	2. IGNORE AT FIRST, SINCE MANY TIMES THIS WILL CURE THE PROBLEM. IF DISRUPTIONS CONTINUE, REMEMBER THE GUIDELINES INVOLVED: • HANDLE THE PROBLEM EARLY • NEVER EMBARRASS OR "PUT DOWN THE TROUBLEMAKER" IN FRONT OF THE GROUP • NEVER LOSE YOUR TEMPER DURING THE DISRUPTION HANDLE THE PROBLEM QUICKLY AND DELICATELY
Non-Verbal Clues	
Symptoms	Remedial Action Plan
1. ABSOLUTE SILENCE FROM AUDIENCE, COUPLED WITH NONVERBAL GESTURES RANGING FROM PURE BOREDOM TO ANNOYANCE TO MILD HOSTILITY	1. AUDIENCE OBVIOUSLY "TURNED OFF" FOR WHATEVER REASON. BEGIN PROBING IMMEDIATELY — BOTH WITH SELECTED INDIVIDUALS AND (WHERE APPROPRIATE), "CHALLENGE" THE GROUP TO UNEARTH A BETTER DEFINITION THAN THE ONE YOU GAVE... A MORE CONCISE EXPLANATION THAN THAT DISPLAYED IN AN OVERHEAD TRANSPARENCY, ETC.
2. "ZOMBIE" PARTICIPANTS: THE DESCRIPTION HERE DOES NOT EMANATE FROM ANY VOODO CULTURE, BUT DESCRIBES AN AUDIENCE MEMBER WHO REACTS IN THIS MANNER: • HE/SHE IS LIVING, BREATHING AND OBVIOUSLY ALIVE, BUT THAT IS WHERE THEIR PRESENCE STOPS • ALTHOUGH THEY ARE TAKING UP PHYSICAL SPACE, NOTHING ELSE IS HAPPENING... THEIR EYES ARE GLASSY, THEIR HEADS STAY IN ONE POSITION FOR LONG INTERVALS, THEY RARELY BLINK, AND ONE OFTEN WONDERS IF THEY ARE TRULY ALIVE DURING YOUR TALK!	2A. QUICK ACTION IS CALLED FOR! BUT DO IT DISCREETLY. IF THE PERSON IS HALF-ASLEEP, NEVER CALL ON HIM/HER DIRECTLY, SINCE THIS WILL ONLY EMBARRASS OR STARTLE THE INDIVIDUAL. THE SKILL IS TO CALL ON THE PERSON SITTING ON EITHER SIDE OF THE "ZOMBIE." DONE OVER SEVERAL MINUTES, THIS INDIVIDUAL IS BOUND TO EMERGE FROM HIS TRANCE. ONCE THIS IS NOTED, PROBE HIM SEVERAL TIMES (STARTING WITH WHAT YOU KNOW WILL BE EASY RESPONSES) AND WORK UP FROM THERE.

FIGURE 12-3:
Audience Reaction Strategy Checklist (Filled-in Sample of Form 10)

presentations, they provide a valuable *reference of lessons learned*, and (at a later date) offer a *rich source of tips and techniques for use in coaching someone else!*

As just one example, let's take the case of the "zombie" participant. Knowing in advance how to spot the problem, then employing the correct remedial action that was taken, puts the speaker in a strong position to handle the situation when (and if) it should arise again in future talks.

Putting the Four Steps to Work For You

You are now ready to put the four steps to work for you. Follow the four steps outlined in this chapter:

1. Select a topic for your first talk.
2. Determine whom you would prefer as a coach, then review the critiquing procedures that will be required.
   (Note: If possible, have your coach read Chapter 12 also. In addition, an important double benefit is available here. By going through this entire workbook together, at the conclusion of each chapter, your roles can be reversed, with you acting as coach, and vice versa.)
3. Complete your first talk, having your coach critique you via the evaluation checklist (Form 8).
4. Transfer appropriate comments from the evaluation checklist to the Checklist for Personal Improvement (Form 9).

Post-Graduate Checklist

Upon completion of this chapter, you will have successfully worked your way through the essential elements of preparing and delivering high quality presentations. At this point, you should be well along the road to becoming a truly professional speaker.

Now would be the ideal time to pause and reflect for a few moments on your new level of expertise as compared to the potential of even higher peaks of performance during business presentations. The adage of "practice makes perfect" was never more appropriate for the art of delivering an effective presentation.

In effect, you have now "graduated" from this course, but as you know, the learning process never stops. In that regard, for whatever new skill level you have reached, it would be prudent now to be somewhat introspective on those techniques which you have mastered well . . . together with skills that would benefit from further improvement. Let's take a closer look at the sample filled-in checklist (Figure 12-4) and see how this would work in the real world.

Note that the form is divided into two sections. The first deals with techniques that you have mastered quite well, while the second focuses upon areas requiring additional improvement. Take a moment now and complete Part A. Once a skill has been listed, reflect upon how you can become even more proficient at it. For example, you might list the *use of pauses* as one technique which has greatly aided your efficiency on the platform. Upon reflection, you realize that if these pauses were coupled with a higher degree of *voice modulation*, it would become even more effective. Put another way, as an attention-getting device, or to accentuate a point, the speaker would maintain a steady voice level for a few moments . . . pause . . . then resume (for a few seconds) in a much *louder* (or softer) voice depending upon the mood one wished to create.

Once you have listed several of these techniques, it's time to move on to Part B, which asks you to list areas requiring additional corrective action. Here is where your coach could be of especially valuable help in pinpointing *specific* areas that still required work.

For example, let's say that you have always been plagued by nervousness. For the first few presentations, you were inwardly terrified and this unfortunate condition was highly visible to the audience in the form of vocalized pauses (heavy use of 'UHHhh's' and "MMMmmm's") and an undue reliance on *reading* notes, instead of speaking directly to the audience. Although the situation has improved somewhat since your earlier talks, it's clear that more help is required.

Upon reflection, you realize that better use of the *Summary Key Point Planner* (with its bulleted-point format), and more reliance on preparing flip-charts in advance (instead of writing them out during the talk) would help to achieve a smoother flow of the presentation, and this in itself would be a definite aid in reducing nervousness!

The post-graduate checklist is *not* the perfect fail-safe mechanism to automatically guarantee that you will become a more proficient speaker. However, it has been proven by many speakers, who have undertaken the same type of training (as you have via this workbook), that it is a very worthwhile exercise to complete.

Again, if you have been working with a coach throughout this program, this exercise (including the remedial action to be taken) should only take a few moments of your time. If no coach is available to you, don't be discouraged. The exercise will be slightly harder to do since one must be certain that they have been *completely objective*. But if the exercise is done properly, the benefit will be the same as with the coach/partner relationship.

Finally, always make certain that you include the *date* that the remedial action will be taken . . . *and stick to it!* If the date does not reflect the actual time that a formal talk will be given, it should be the time when you intend to practice in front of a video camera, alone in front of a mirror, or perhaps a confidential session with your coach.

The main point is to do it!

POST GRADUATE CHECKLIST

Date: _11/16/87_

A) Techniques That I Now Excel At	How Can They Be Further Improved	Date It Will Be Done
Use of pauses	Couple with a higher degree of voice modulation	Attempt this with planned talk on Business Cycles scheduled for Dec. 5th
Good eye contact	Make even more effective with continued slow, even "eye sweep" of entire room	Dec. 5th Business Presentation

B) Platform Skill That Requires Further Strengthening	Specific Steps to Accomplish This	Date It Will Be Done
Stop relying on use of vocalized pauses (uhhs, uhms)	Better use of Presentation Planner (more reliance on bullet format)	Start preparing Planner, week 11/28 for 12/5 talk
Avoid reading notes verbatim	Must prepare all my flipcharts in advance (don't wait until morning of presentation)	Begin creating flipcharts on 11/28

FIGURE 12-4:
Post-Graduate Checklist (Filled-in Sample of Form 11)

CHAPTER 13

How to Deliver
A Winning "High-Tech" Presentation

This chapter will illustrate the process of creating a high-tech business presentation. Then (following the format in Chapter 7) a specific example of a talk on a high-tech subject will be presented in a step-by-step fashion.

High-Tech Audio-Visual Logistics

As the computer and word processor revolutionized the process of written communication (sometimes referred to as *desktop publishing*), it has also extended itself into the art of creating graphics and visuals for use in business presentations of all types.

While this capability of enhanced audio-visual design and flexibility brings numerous benefits to a speaker, at the same time certain basic cautions must be observed. Just as a person's writing style doesn't automatically improve with the use of a word-processor and laser-printer, so it is with computer graphics. If not planned properly, the same boring slides and transparencies will be produced . . . except perhaps with greater speed (and corresponding cost) than the "old" method.

Due to the wide acceptance of computer graphics, virtually all major data-processing organizations now offer a range of equipment to fit every requirement (and pocketbook). One only has to visit a computer store to see companies like IBM, Apple, Xerox, 3M, Kodak and Hewlett-Packard to note how extensive the hardware list really is. Frequent business speakers (while having the capability of creating visuals on just about any type of personal computer) usually prefer to work with oversize color monitors coupled with sophisticated video graphic cards and increased memory capability to handle the more complicated scenarios. Regarding selection, it's generally a question of the increased cost of the equipment versus the need involved.

The computer output for graphics is equally dazzling. In most cases, the speaker can elect to have the final visual version not only in the traditional 35mm color slides or overhead transparencies (with the accompanying hard-copy text for use as handouts or participant text material), but also in video or electronic imaging format.

In a broad sense, the software package employed will drive the degree of sophistication that can be achieved by the hardware system. Users have a choice of relatively inexpensive software programs for such basic computer graphics as graphs, bar charts, and indexes. Going up the ladder in price, the costlier software package enables the user to combine the graphics and text in a fully integrated manner.

As expected, many service bureaus are making these specialized types of production assistance available. The market for this should continue to grow at a rapid rate, since there are many organizations that would prefer to have outside production experts handling the logistics—whether the motive be lack of time, lack of required expertise, or simply not being able to justify buying and maintaining their own systems based on limited usage.

Service Bureaus vs. In-House Production

The following are some pro and con factors:

Let's assume that you have the ability to create images in-house with some type of desktop presentation equipment. Following simple logic, you now have two choices on how to obtain the required output (whether it be in the form of overhead transparencies, 35mm slides, or prints).

1. Do the production in-house
2. Use an outside service bureau facility.

Let's look at some key factors for each choice.

1. In-House Production

    A. As a first caveat, it's vital to make certain that the software used will be compatible with the hardware system you will require (fortunately, the majority of software systems specify the required interfaces for specific output options).

    B. Unfortunately (at the time this text is being written) no one type of output system can produce both slides and overheads. For *slide production,* a film recorder is needed . . . and these can range in cost from $1,500 up to

$18,000–20,000. The price paid is generally based on degree of color sharpness and resolution required by the presenter. Once the recorder (which works somewhat like a camera) completes the imaging, the film can be processed at any photography lab and then printed as 35mm slides. Factors coming into play when considering purchase of a recorder would heavily focus on:

- Frequency of use
- Degree of slide quality required
- Availability of a trained in-house technician

C. To produce overhead transparencies, a suitable type printer is required. Three type of printers are now available.

- *The Dot Matrix Printer:*
  Two main characteristics are that they are generally inexpensive (starting at approximately $250) and fast (some models can print over 200 characters per second—referred to as *cps*). As such, they are most suitable for operations that require high-speed volume and where sharp imaging is not required.

- *Daisywheel:*
  Using a spoked print wheel to imprint upon ribbon, this process is ideal for most word processing applications. Advantages are in its high quality output and affordability—with prices starting in the $400–500 range. A major disadvantage lies in its slow speed (generally 25 to 40 cps).

- *Laser Printers:*
  Most suitable for creating overhead transparencies, laser printers offer high resolution, concise graphics and premier-quality word processing output. Costs generally run under $1,800 (although more sophisticated models are well over $2,000).

For color printing, dot matrix printers will cost from $500 to $3,000. The highest quality output and color variety are obtained from color lasers, but with price tags of around $20,000–25,000. Heavy in-house use, coupled with professional quality required, is the main justification for their purchase.

2. Outside Service Bureaus

These facilities generally offer the flexibility of being able to produce prints, overheads, and slides within 24 to 48 hours, upon receipt of the customer's files via modem. While prices can vary quite widely, an outside service bureau will generally charge:

- $10–25 each for a 35mm color slide (basic cardboard mount)
- $5–20 each for overhead transparencies

Based on these numbers, it would appear that service bureaus are geared for presenters who require only minimum volumes on an occasional basis, and are therefore not able to justify the hardware expense involved. Bear in mind, however, that before any type of decision is reached, a methodical analysis of all the pros and cons involved is a *must*. What's logical for one company or speaker may be entirely inappropriate for another. Careful analysis of cost versus usage is the key here.

Now that we have highlighted some of the high-tech logistics available in creating a business presentation, let's focus on a real-world talk based on a technical subject.

Master Account Tracking System (MATS)

Category

This particular presentation covers all three categories—i.e., to inform, motivate, and persuade.

What to Emphasize

Major emphasis:

- Keeping the talk fast-paced and interesting (especially during the main body where the technical info is being introduced)
- Starting with early WIFM's and maintaining a continuous stream of benefits throughout the presentation
- Being as factual as possible without being dry. (Remember that the audience can be a bit cynical about being promised a technical system only to be disappointed later on, when it could possibly fail to live up to stated expectations.)
- Due to technical nature of subject, creating lively/interesting visuals yet keeping talk simple, i.e., not unduly complicated for the average person in the audience. (This is a perfect example of the benefits of knowing your audience in advance.)

Secondary emphasis:

- Present the material in a highly factual manner while at the same time heavily stressing additional systems benefits, i.e., goal setting, bonus planning, new account tracking, and projection analysis capability

Pitfalls to Avoid

During the presentation, attention should be paid to the following caution areas:

- Getting too technical and thereby losing part (or the majority) of the audience
- Inadvertently appearing too aloof (mechanical) and, without meaning to, "talking down" to your audience

- Not structuring the talk to allow sufficient time at the conclusion for questions, and being conscious of the different levels of understanding in the audience.

Speaker Tips:

- When presenting a very technical subject (such as a new data reporting system), be aware that some people remain cynical about data-processing in general.
- With a typical nontechnical audience, there is bound to be some confusion and possible misinterpretation to what you are saying. Accordingly, keep checking for understanding.
- In order to reach your objective successfully, you must walk the very fine line between being a bit simplistic, yet technical enough for the average person to comprehend the main elements of the presentation.
- Try to keep a relaxed (yet firm) body language posture throughout the talk.
- Barring unforeseen circumstances, always avoid use of humor during technical presentations. In most cases, its inappropriate.
- And *always* be prepared (anticipate) the questions that probably will arise as a result of your talk.

The Framework:

Pre-planning: Since your talk will include all three categories (inform, motivate, and persuade) it is essential to keep the presentation as factual as necessary, but also stimulating and interesting. Key points to bear in mind:

- If possible, try to meet (and mingle) with as many of your audience as possible *prior* to the presentation. This will be an effective "ice-breaker" for those who do not know you, and a good reinforcement for the others.
- A strong effective opening will be essential for this type of talk.
- Since you already know that the audience will be relatively small (probably around 10–14 people) you may want to consider handling questions as they arise (rather than holding all of them to the end). Be prepared to be flexible on this point, and use your judgment.
- Make certain that you have a strong arsenal of WIFM's for this type of technical presentation (you will probably need them to help create and maintain interest).
- Careful selection of the visuals to be used is key. In general, for a high-tech

talk, the appropriate visuals can be a tremendous plus in making the presentation a success.

Attention/Interest:

This can be accomplished by carefully selecting connectors that highlight:

- A system that, for the first time, will base a salesperson's compensation on performance—instead of just salary alone.
- A heavy benefit to sales management will be the ability (also for the first time) to properly set sales quotas and goals for the field sales rep.
- For administrative management, the system will track profitability of the various products and of major accounts throughout the country.

Main Body:

Key points to cover:

- A reinforcement of why the system is needed
- How the system will work
- Overview of the input sources required
- Field responsibility for data input (type, format, and frequency)
- Home office responsibility for system coordination
- What the system will produce in the form of hard data
- Summary of benefits to accounts, sales force, and the home office management team

Desire and Action:

The Power Close should include such items as:

- A timetable for implementation (what's going to happen when)
- A summary of the forms that will be required for data input, coupled with a scheduled date for sales force training on how to implement system data
- A restatement of benefits for all concerned including a new beginning in company growth and profitability—as a team effort of all concerned.
- A conclusion, that encourages the audience to ask any questions (or express any concerns) that haven't been addressed up to now

Forms and Other Aids to Use

In addition to the Key Point Summarizer, the following forms and figures should help make preparing this type of talk easier:

- Strategy Classification Chart (Figure 1-1)
- Presentation Classification Model (Figure 1-2)
- Pretalk Room Checklist (Figure 1-3)

Background Data for Sample Presentation

Imperial Products Ltd. is a custom manufacturer and distributor of "top-of-the-line" automobile covers for all late model U.S. and foreign sports cars. The product is sold mainly to selected automotive jobbers and (in certain areas of the country) to carefully chosen upscale auto-supply stores in affluent marketing areas. The product is sold through a national sales force, all of whom are compensated on a straight salary basis (plus travel expenses). This compensation plan is considered grossly unfair by the entire sales force, and has been a continuing source of friction between salespeople and middle-management.

At the year-end sales meeting, the firm's general manager requested Laura Langley (head of Imperial's Data Processing Center in San Diego) to talk to the company's sales management and marketing team about the newly developed MATS program (Master Account Tracking System). If the system performs to stated specifications for the first time, the firm's major accounts would be able to be tracked not only by unit and model sales, but (just as importantly) by account profitability. In addition, this new data system would provide the added benefit of supplying statistics for a proposed (and much needed) revised compensation plan for the sales force, and its regional sales management team.

Unfortunately, there was bound to be a high degree of cynicism from all concerned, since (during the past three years) similar systems had been promised, but nothing ever developed.

Special Note: In preparing her technical presentation, Laura relied on high-tech methodology to produce the supporting visuals needed for an effective talk.

Knowing her audience for the presentation (the approximate 10–12 member sales management/marketing team) and the conference room that would be used, she decided on the following technique:

The first part of her presentation (the opener) was designed around a series of fast-moving slides that would set the mood and pace of her presentation. This was done by employing two slide projectors in sync, displayed on a rear screen projection system within the room she would speak in. For added effect, the connector to the main body would be displayed on a pre-drawn flipchart.

The main body (being technical in nature) would center around highly colorful (but simple in concept) overhead transparencies.

The ending (power close), which would include a summary of the key presentation points, would be shown back on the rear screen projection unit via a return to the 35mm slide format.

Just three days prior to the talk Laura learned that her presentation would be videotaped and (via teleconferencing) would be shown simultaneously in the firm's two regional distribution centers located in Chicago, Illinois, and Buffalo, New York. Last (but certainly not least) it was also mentioned to her by Imperial's President (Chuck Olsen) that the parent company (Butterworth and Sandler located in London) had requested a copy of the videotape for viewing by their Board of Managers.

It struck Laura that what she had originally perceived as a low-keyed talk on a normally dull subject was now turning into a major presentation.

Truly an exciting challenge!

Accordingly, after completing the Key Point Summarizer and sketching the rough outlines of the visuals, Laura's secretary was able to design these via her desktop computer. After completing same (and to save time) this was sent via modem to a local service bureau located near the San Francisco meeting site for production. While this developmental effort was occurring, Laura transmitted specific meeting planning requirements to the conference center via Fax (as shown in Figure 13-1)

A real-world example of preparing a technical presentation using high-tech (but readily available) production methods! Figure 13-2 shows how Laura used the Key Point Summarizer to prepare her presentation.

Sample Power Openers

"Good morning! It's nice to be here with all of you. Now . . . I know your time is extremely valuable, so I'll come right to the point. In the next 30 minutes, I plan to illustrate a new Master Account Tracking System that will directly benefit each person in this room. How's that for a challenge? Now . . . let's get started!"

and

"It seems we inherited lots of problems along our road to success. For one thing, our current sales force compensation plan is both antiquated and unfair. On top of that we really have no way to track account profitability, or for that matter even set reasonable performance goals on field sales! But . . . we believe all of this can now be changed for the better, and I'm here today to show each of you how this can be accomplished. Fair enough?"

Sample Connector

"What you will now see demonstrated is a new system that has been specifically designed to deliver us out of this mess . . . once and for all. As we go through each new innovation that MATS will bring, we'll contrast it point by point to the weaknesses of the current system and how we intend to correct it."

Sample Main Body Selections

"As a starter, we will look at a complete system overview. This will begin with a simplified view of all the integral components that are needed to make the system operational. After that we'll review the data input required from the field, look at how the home office will do the necessary coordination, and (most importantly) the new system output reports that will help everyone in this room do their jobs better."

and

"As you will note from the overhead, the system directly links both our gross and net sales (by product) to all key jobbers and major accounts—and does so on a monthly and quarterly basis. This one feature alone will give you the capability of determining account

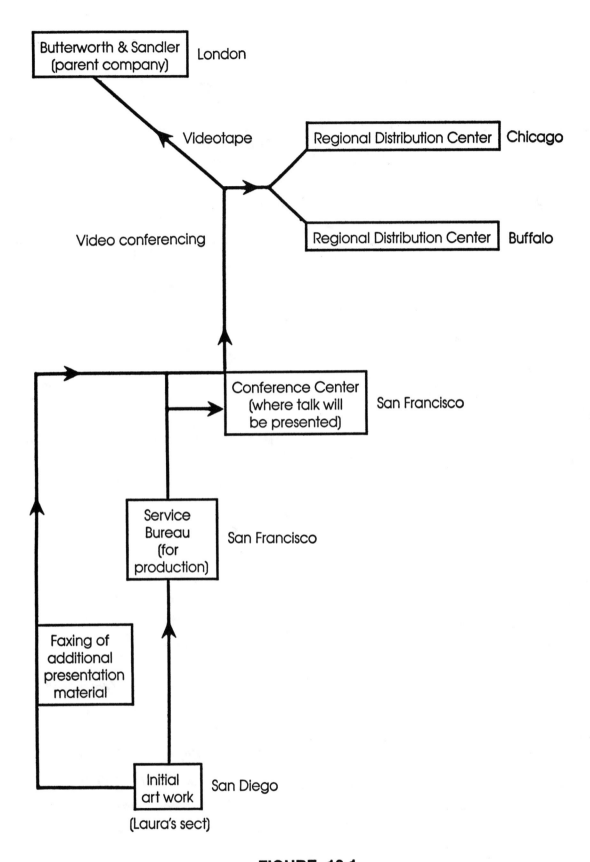

FIGURE 13-1

KEY POINT SUMMARIZER

TITLE OF PRESENTATION: _Master Account Tracking System (MATS)_
DATE GIVEN: _January 12, 1989_
ANTICIPATED DURATION: _35-40 minutes_
FORMAL INTRODUCTION: ___ YES ___ NO   INFORMAL INTRODUCTION: ___ YES ___ NO
ROOM DIMENSIONS: _50' x 60' (app)_   AUDIENCE SIZE: _____
FAMILIAR WITH AUDIENCE? ✔ YES ___ NO
TYPE OF AUDIO VISUAL AIDS PLANNED: _1_ FLIPCHART(S)   ✔ TRANSPARENCY(IES)
                                      ✔ 35MM SLIDE(S)   ✔ VIDEOTAPE
                                      ✔ HANDOUTS   _____ OTHER

SUMMARY POINTS	VISUAL AIDS
1. Power Opener: _INTRO_ • _You've heard this before - but new system will solve many problems_ • _During next 25 minutes - will prove this to you_ • _Request you keep an open mind_ • _This presentation could be most important part of this entire sales meeting_	_SLIDE SEQUENCE_ _Slide #1 & #2 (Title shot, in synch)_ _#3 (New Beginning) #4 (We've Done It)_ _Slides #5 & 6 (Now, Let's Prove It) synch_ _Slides #7 & 8 (Keep an Open Mind) synch_ _Slide #9 (We Know the Challenge)_ _Slide #10 (We also Know the Obstacles)_ _Slides #11 & 12 (Let's Get Started!) synch_
2. Connector: _BENEFITS OF MATS:_ • _Compensation to be based on performance_ • _Will establish needed quotas and goals_ • _Can now track product/account profitability with all major customers_ • _Should increase field sales force motivation/reduce turnover/increase sales_	_FLIPCHART PAGE SEQUENCE_ _Page 1 Title (Benefits of MATS)_ _Page 2 Quotas and Goals_ _Page 3 Track Product/Account Profitability with all major customers_ _Page 4 - Increase Motivation_ _ - Reduce Turnover_ _ - Increase Sales_

FIGURE 13-2:
Master Account Tracking System (MATS)
(Filled in Sample of Summarizer)

KEY POINT SUMMARIZER (Continued)

TITLE OF PRESENTATION: *Master Account Tracking System (MATS)*
DATE GIVEN: *January 12, 1989*

SUMMARY POINTS	VISUAL AIDS
3. *Main Body:*	TRANSPARENCY SEQUENCE
SYSTEM OVERVIEW	#1 Main Heading
• Integral components	#2 • Components involved
• Relationship of system to jobbers and major accounts	• System relationships
• Tie in to home office/marketing data requirements	• Home office coordination
DATA INPUT REQUIREMENTS	#3 Main Heading
• Key is field sales rep	#4 • Sales rep-key to success
• Separate forms needed for jobbers and direct accounts	• Forms required
• Examples of both forms	#5 • Both forms displayed side by side
• Procedure for form completion and distribution	#6 • Procedure for jobber form
	• Procedure for D.A. form
HOME OFFICE REQUIREMENTS	#7 Main Heading
• System coordinator	#8 • Coordination required
• Distribution of reports	• Info distribution
• Continuous validation of data	• Validation required
SYSTEM OUTPUT	#9 Main Heading
• Net monthy sales to jobbers/direct accounts	#10 • Monthly reports
• Profitability analysis for both	• Profitability by account
• Goals vs. sales achievement by individual reps	#11 • Goals/Sales analysis
• Sales forecasting by account/region	• Forecasting methodology

FIGURE 13-2:
(continued)

TITLE OF PRESENTATION: *Master Account Tracking System (MATS)*
DATE GIVEN: *January 12, 1989*

SUMMARY POINTS	VISUAL AIDS
4. Power Close:	SLIDE SEQUENCE
TIMETABLE FOR IMPLEMENTATION	Slide #13 Title Shot
• *Sales Management approval next week (January 18th)*	#14 (Jan. 18 - Sales Management)
• *Divisional approval February 1ˢᵗ*	#15 (Feb. 1 - Divisional)
• *Initial forms/input from field due February 15*	#16 (Feb. 15 - Field Input Due)
• *System operational by March 15*	Synch
TRAINING	#17 (March 15 - Operational)
• *Field training on forms/data input to begin immediately after management approval*	#18 Title Shot
	#19 (Field Training Support)
RESTATEMENT OF BENEFITS	#20 Title Shot
• *Better tracking and profitability analysis*	#21 (Better Account Tracking)
	#22 (Profitability Analysis)
• *More equitable compensation*	#23 (Much Fairer Comp. System)
• *Systemized goal setting/forecasting*	#24 (More effective goal/setting and setting and forecasting)
REQUESTING COMMITMENT	Synch
• *Need support of all concerned*	#25 (You are Key to Success!)
• *Take questions*	#26 (Everyone's Help Needed)
	#27 (Thanks in Advance for Support)
	#28 (Questions, anyone?)

FIGURE 13-2:
(continued)

KEY POINT SUMMARIZER (Continued)

TITLE OF PRESENTATION: _Master Account Tracking System (MATS)_

DATE GIVEN: _January 12, 1989_

	Possible Audience Questions	Appropriate Responses
1.	"Sounds good - but heard this before... why is this different when others failed?"	1. No guarantee but much more research done and we now have commitment from all concerned to make it work.
2.	"Last system failed since key person pulled off project two weeks later— what are your plans?"	2. As project manager, I will stay with system for at least 12 months – have management's full support.
3.	"Impressed with system but how about cost? And what about additional staff expense involved?"	3. All costs fully approved by mgmt., and in fact, accrued from last year's budget. There will be no additional staff required to implement and maintain.
4.	"How much additional time is needed for paper work process?"	4. Minimal – less than 30 minutes per day – we've allowed one month for this phase.
5.	"Like idea of tying goal setting/performance to a system, but need to know more about this."	5. Definitely a key issue – we've allowed time for a specific presentation on this later today.

FIGURE 13-2:
(continued)

profitability, build effective sales forecasts, and set performance goals for each salesperson. Now, how's that for a quantum leap from the 'stone age' to the twentieth century!"

Sample Power Close

"We have operated for the past three years with a poorly designed data system. Your complaints were quite justified . . . and we listened carefully. After a lot of hard work, research, and dollars spent, we believe that this new system will correct the situation. But when all is said and done, unless we have the support of everyone in this room, we are probably doomed to failure.

"But . . . this will not happen since I know each of you can be counted upon to assist in this effort! Now, we've covered a tremendous amount of ground in a very short time. So I'm sure you have many questions.

"Let's hear them. I welcome all of your thoughts and ideas!"

Chapter Summary

This final chapter highlighted both the hardware and software required to produce the audio-visual support for a business presentation. As we have seen, there are no definite answers available at this juncture. It's basically up to each organization to determine whether it's more feasible to have in-house production capability or to employ services of an outside center.

To round out the chapter, we then illustrated a typical high-tech presentation where the speaker used a few of the techniques described earlier in the section.

If you've learned nothing else from this workbook, it should be that *planning is the key for any effective presentation.*

Finally, it may interest the reader to know that the talk prepared by Laura Langley (a fictitious name) was partially drawn from a real-world example. As it turned out, after all the required preparations, Laura became ill the night before. Her assistant (who was groomed for the talk "just in case") had to take over with only a few hours notice . . . and did actually very well.

Wishing you the best of luck in all of your future business presentations.

APPENDIX

FORM 1   **PRETALK ROOM CHECKLIST**

Location/Date of Presentation: _____ **Today's Date:** _____

Item	Yes	No	Comments
Part I—Environment/room layout Can be controlled by speaker?			
• Heating			
• Air Conditioning			
• Ventilation (blowers)			
• Lighting			
– Direct			
– Indirect			
– On podium			
– In main seating area			
• Will a podium be used?			
– Table			
– Standing lectern			
– Other?			
• Acoustics satisfactory?			
• Is audience seating arrange- ment suitable for your talk? (i.e., auditorium style, U-shaped, individual tables, schoolroom style, etc.)			
– If not, what can be done about it?			
• If required, is a public address system available?			
– Microphones			
– Lavalier microphone			

Part II—Audiovisual logistics
• Equipment source
  – Being supplied by instructor,
    and/or in-house facility?			

FORM 1 *(Continued)*

Location/Date of Presentation: _____ Today's Date: _____

Item	Yes	No	Comments
– If supplied by outside vendor, • Is equipment insured			
• Will it be delivered in sufficient time to check-out properly?			
• Can equipment be operated by the speaker, or is a trained technician required? Other?			
• Audio-visual aids – Being prepared in-house?			
– By an outside firm?			
– Chance to review before presentation?			
– Have all visuals been selected?			
– To match the specific presentation requirements?			

Part III—Miscellaneous
  • Liaison resource
   – Person to contact for assistance			

– Availability before and during talk			
• Food source – Name of person coordinating			
– Any special restrictions necessary?			
• Need for smoking/non-smoking sections?			
• Other factors			
–			
–			
–			

FORM 2   KEY POINT SUMMARIZER

TITLE OF PRESENTATION: _____

DATE GIVEN: _____

ANTICIPATED DURATION: _____

FORMAL INTRODUCTION: ___ YES ___ NO   INFORMAL INTRODUCTION: ___ YES ___ NO

ROOM DIMENSIONS: _____   AUDIENCE SIZE: _____

FAMILIAR WITH AUDIENCE? ___ YES ___ NO

TYPE OF AUDIO VISUAL AIDS PLANNED: ___ FLIPCHART(S)   ___ TRANSPARENCY(IES)

                                          ___ 35MM SLIDE(S)   ___ VIDEOTAPE

                                          ___ HANDOUTS   _____ OTHER

SUMMARY POINTS	VISUAL AIDS
1. *Power Opener:*	
2. *Connector:*	

KEY POINT SUMMARIZER (*Continued*)

TITLE OF PRESENTATION: _____

DATE GIVEN: _____

SUMMARY POINTS	VISUAL AIDS
3. *Main Body:*	

TITLE OF PRESENTATION: _____

DATE GIVEN: _____

SUMMARY POINTS	VISUAL AIDS
4. *Power Close:*	

KEY POINT SUMMARIZER (*Continued*)

TITLE OF PRESENTATION: _____

DATE GIVEN: _____

	Possible Audience Questions	Appropriate Responses
1.		
2.		
3.		
4.		
5.		

FORM 3

EFFECTIVE PRESENTATION TRAITS

TRAIT	ROLE MODEL	HOW EXHIBITED
Strong presence		
Audience empathy		
An effective opening		
Good eye contact		
Sincerity		
Enthusiasm		
Effective gestures		
No apparent nervousness		
Good voice control		
Appropriate dress		
Persuasive close		

FORM 4

CHECKLIST OF APPROPRIATE SKILLS FOR FOLLOW UP

Date talk(s) given ——— ——— ———

Date checklist completed ———

Trait/Skill	I need to improve	I perform satisfactorily	Not certain
Strong presence			
Audience empathy			
Effective opening			
Good eye contact			
Sincerity			
Enthusiasm			
Effective gestures			
Nervousness			
Voice control			
Appropriate dress			
Persuasive close			

FORM 5

FOLLOW-UP ACTION GUIDE

Skill Areas Requiring Correction	Remedial Action to be Taken During			Date
	Talk #1 Date:	Talk #2 Date:	Talk #3 Date:	Results Obtained

FORM 6   AUDIOVISUAL SUPPORT CHECKLIST

Location of Presentation: _____ Today's Date: _____
Date of Presentation: _____ Room Size: _____
Acoustic Level (Excellent, Average, Poor): _____
Room Lighting: (a) Can Be Easily Controlled: _____ (Yes) _____ (No)
                   (b) Go From Light To Dark Quickly: _____ (Yes) _____ (No)
                   (c) Controlled By Speaker: _____ (Yes) _____ (No)

Item	Usage			Availability		
	Yes	No	Uncertain	Have	Need to Rent	Comments
Standing Floor Microphone						
Lavalier Microphone						
Built-In Public Address System						
Flipchart(s)						
Blackboard(s)						
Standing Floor Podium						
Table Podium						
35mm Slide Projector						
16mm Projector						
8mm Projector						
Cassette Recorder/Playback						
Video Camera						
Video Record/Playback Deck						
Video Monitor						
Overhead Projector						
Pointer (For Speaker)						
Extension Cords						
Spare Equipment Bulbs						

FORM 7

CHECKLIST FOR HANDLING DISRUPTIONS

Date of Planned Talk: _____

Type	Individual's Name	Countermeasures to be Employed
Chatterbox		
Overly Dependent		
Superiority		
V.I.P.		
Chronic Complainer		
Authority Figure		

FORM 8   COACH EVALUATION CHECKLIST

Speaker: _____   Coach: _____

Title of Talk: _____

Date: _____   Audience Size: _____

Location: _____   Planned Length of Talk _____

Type of Audio-Visual Used _____   Starting Time _____ Ending Time _____

Category	Satisfactory	Needs Improvement
Presentation format Well organized opening		
Good continuity		
Clear points made		
Effective ending		
Personal dynamics Enthusiastic		
Persuasive		
Good presence		
In control		
Mannerisms Nervousness		
Distracting gestures		
Voice projection		
Modulation		
Tone		
(other)		
Eyes Maintained audience contact		
Occasional sweep		
(other)		
Miscellaneous		

FORM 9   CHECKLIST FOR PERSONAL IMPROVEMENT

Category	Comments Noted	Personal Reaction
Presentation format Well organized opening		
Good continuity		
Clear points made		
Effective ending		
Personal Dynamics Enthusiastic		
Persuasive		
Good presence		
In control		
Mannerisms Nervousness		
Distracting gestures		
Voice projection		
Modulation		
Tone		
(other)		
Eyes Maintained audience contact		
Occasional sweep		
(other)		
Miscellaneous		

FORM 10

AUDIENCE REACTION STRATEGY CHECKLIST	
Verbal Clues	
Symptoms	Remedial Action Plan
1.	1.
2.	2.
3.	3.
4	4.
Non-Verbal Clues	
Symptoms	Remedial Action Plan
1.	1.
2.	2.
3.	3.
4.	4.

FORM 11   **POST GRADUATE CHECKLIST**

Date: _____

A) Techniques That I Now Excel At	How Can They Be Further Improved	Date It Will Be Done

B) Platform Skill That Requires Further Strengthening	Specific Steps to Accomplish This	Date It Will Be Done

Notes

Notes

Notes

Notes

Notes

Notes

Notes